LECTURE NOTES

a professor's
inside guide to
college success

Philip Freeman, PhD

TEN SPEED PRESS
Berkeley

For my students

All rights reserved.
Published in the United States by Ten Speed Press, an imprint of the
Crown Publishing Group, a division of Random House, Inc., New York.
www.crownpublishing.com
www.tenspeed.com

Ten Speed Press and the Ten Speed Press colophon are
registered trademarks of Random House, Inc.

Library of Congress Cataloging-in-Publication Data
Freeman, Philip, 1961–
Lecture notes : a professor's inside guide to college
success / Philip Freeman. — 1st ed.
p. cm.
Includes bibliographical references and index.
ISBN 978-1-58008-754-4 (alk. paper)
1. College student orientation. 2. Study skills. I. Title.
LB2343.3.F74 2010
378.1'70281—dc22
2009038120

ISBN-13: 978-1-58008-754-4

Printed in the United States of America

Cover and text design by Katy Brown
Cover photo © Stephen Stickler / Corbis

10 9 8 7 6 5 4 3 2 1

First Edition

contents

preface

This is not a book about getting into a good college or living with a crazy roommate. It is not a guide to finding scholarship money or cooking lasagna in your dorm room without setting off the fire alarm. This is instead a handbook for getting along with and profiting from the most important people in your life during your college years—your professors.

Sure, college is about making friendships that will last a lifetime and developing yourself as an independent adult, but unless you make your professors and what you can learn from them your prime focus, you are going to waste an amazing amount of time and money over the next few years.

What I offer you in this short book is a view from the other side of the lectern. I've taught hundreds of students at schools large and small. Sadly, I've seen many of these bright students make the same mistakes in dealing with their professors and the classes they teach. You can, however, avoid these mistakes in your own college career by following a few commonsense tips and techniques.

Many thanks to all those who helped me write this book, but especially to my students at Harvard University, Boston University, Washington University, and Luther College. I always believed that being a college professor would be the best job in the world—and you proved me right.

THE THREE RULES FOR COLLEGE SUCCESS

College is hard, but the rules for college success are simple. The trick is, even though the rules are simple in theory, they are often very difficult in practice. But, here's my official college professor's guarantee: If you consistently and conscientiously follow these rules throughout your college years, you will ace your courses, impress your friends and family, and have prospective employers or graduate schools begging you to walk through their doors.

FIRST RULE: GO TO CLASS

Ever since your first day of kindergarten, when your mom tearfully sent you off to school with a kiss and a peanut butter and jelly sandwich, everyone has been telling you that you have to go to school. For thirteen long years you did just that, even when you felt tired, bored, vaguely ill, or whatever excuse you could come up with that day. But guess what? Now that you're in college, no one will make you go to class. You can lie in bed every day until dinner and—although you will probably convince your roommate you have the motivation of a houseplant—no one will really care. The college president will not call your parents nor will most professors bother to track you down.

But your professors will notice. Even in large lecture courses, your absence will become evident by your poor test scores if not by your empty seat. In smaller courses and seminars, skipping classes is like wearing a flashing red sign on your head that says: *Please give me a bad grade.*

Nothing in college is more important than showing up for your classes. And I don't mean just at the beginning of the semester when you're still excited about learning a new subject. I mean at the end of four months when your brain is dead and your body cries out for precious sleep.

I could state the obvious, that if you are not present in class you will miss important material that will help you on tests and maybe even improve your life in some unpredictable way, but you already know that. I could also say that an average hour of class time in college costs you more than tickets to a Broadway play or major league baseball game. Instead, I will simply warn that repeatedly missing classes is one of the surest ways possible to alienate your professors. Most college teachers do indeed fit the image of a kind-hearted figure in tweed who will go out of their way to give a student a helping hand. But blow off their classes and they will have their revenge. No one wants to be ignored. Professors like to think that the students in our classes are actually anxious to hear our words of wisdom. We like to imagine you would cheerfully drag yourself through a raging blizzard just to write down our brilliant thoughts on the Punic Wars or microeconomic theory. So go to class every day, even when you don't want to.

SECOND RULE: READ THE BOOKS

Have you checked out the price of college textbooks? The required books for a single course often cost over a hundred dollars, usually more in classes such as chemistry or literature. Yet, many students let their books collect dust until the night before the big exam, then frantically skim five hundred pages of material. They'd be better off putting their books under their pillows and hoping some of the information would magically seep into their brains. At least then they would get a good night's sleep.

Later, I'll let you in on some proven study techniques that will help you manage the enormous amount of material your professors will assign you. The point now is just that you can't do well in college without reading the books. And I don't mean just perusing a book like you would a magazine article, but really working through material in an organized and productive way. Whether you're doing calculus or Chinese poetry, you have to put your heart into it.

Professors will actually expect you to have read the assigned material for a course. It could be that you'll work through two hundred pages of deadly dull material and none of it will be on the exam. Or that last-minute, single-page handout that you stuffed in your backpack may be the focus of the whole test. You never really know. Sometimes professors will delight in adding something to an exam from an obscure passage just to make sure you did the readings. Once, when I was teaching a class on English vocabulary, I included the word *ponophobia* on the final test for students to define. It had not been mentioned in class nor was it prominent in the book. But it showed me who had done the readings carefully. It means, by the way, "fear of hard work."

THIRD RULE: TALK TO YOUR PROFESSORS

During my first semester of college, I was terrified of my professors. There I was, a freshman just out of high school taking classes from people with a PhD after their names. I thought my job was to quietly take notes and do as well as I could on tests. I would never have dreamed of opening my mouth in class or visiting my professors in their offices to ask a question. Then, one day I was having serious trouble understanding a key concept in my philosophy class, so I worked up the courage to actually approach my professor to ask for help. It turns out he wasn't nearly as scary as I had thought.

If you are going to succeed in college, you must talk to your professors. This might be to ask a question about a lecture point, to get some help on a paper, or just to confess you are hopelessly lost in the course. Professors are there to help you, but the only way we can do that is if we know you have a problem. Not every problem can be easily fixed, but I guarantee it won't get fixed at all unless you sit down and work it out with your professor.

But, learning to talk with your professors is about much more than just sorting out difficulties. Getting to know your teachers in college can benefit you in many ways, though it isn't always easy.

Most professors are shy people. We never sat at the "cool" table in the junior high cafeteria and were not elected homecoming queen or king. We missed all the good parties in college because we had term papers we wanted to finish first. We spent countless hours of graduate school buried in the bowels of some gigantic research library checking footnotes and writing dissertations no one would ever read. And then, all of a sudden, we found ourselves lecturing in front of two hundred energetic college students. It's a frightening situation for anyone.

Almost all professors genuinely like working with and getting to know students—it's just that sometimes we don't know how. Therefore, it will be your job as a student to break down the barriers and get to know your professors. Why should you bother to do this? Two reasons: (1) professors are often fascinating people who will greatly enhance your college experience if you get to know them outside the classroom, and (2) it will improve your grades and future prospects.

Most college professors may be shy, but they've also read more, done more, and been more places than just about any other group you'll ever meet. They've collected fungi samples in Peru, hiked the Great Wall of China, and know all the best coffee houses near the British Museum. They've read Dante and Emily Dickinson and wouldn't dream of missing the weekly *New York Times Book Review*. Even if they haven't done all that, they have a lot to offer if you get to know them.

Getting to know college professors can also make a difference on your final grade in a course. This is a fact few professors like to talk about, but it's true nonetheless. It's much harder to give a bad grade to a student you know than to just another face in the lecture hall. I'm not saying professors will unfairly raise the grades of their favorite students—I've given plenty of poor grades and even failing marks to students I've known well and liked. But when it comes time for us to calculate grades at the end of a semester, those borderline students who have met with us, talked with us, and shown a genuine interest in our subjects have a better chance of a higher grade than unknown students.

Finally, one thing few students think about when starting their college careers is that they will need letters of recommendation from their professors when they apply for jobs or graduate school. These letters are often every bit as important as your transcript, sometimes more. In order for your professors to write effective letters when you apply to law school, we have to know more about you than just your score in our grade book. The only way for this to happen is for you to take the time—over three or more years if possible—to get to know us outside the classroom.

None of this means that you should invite your professors to hang out with you and your buddies down at the local pub. There are boundaries most conscientious professors will not cross as a matter of professional conduct and personal integrity. But, there are plenty of legitimate opportunities to get to know your professors outside of class that most would welcome—office hours, departmental receptions, and campus lectures, to name just a few.

Make it a goal early in your college career to pick at least three professors and develop a professional, but sincere, relationship with them. It will definitely be worth your time.

HIGH SCHOOL VERSUS COLLEGE

I will never forget my first day of college. I had just turned eighteen and was ready to conquer the world. I couldn't wait to put high school behind me and read great books, study with brilliant professors, and discuss ideas with new friends late into the night. As it turned out, college really was wonderful, but it was not what I had imagined. Like most people, my idea of education was shaped by my experiences in high school. I knew college would be harder, of course, but I didn't know exactly how it would work. So, let's consider how the academic side of college is different from high school.

SCHEDULES

If you're like me, you showed up at high school about 8 A.M. every morning and worked there nonstop for seven hours or more. Recess is something they took away in sixth grade, so that by your high school years you were rushing between classrooms with barely enough time to get a drink from the water fountain.

Now comes your first day of college. Most first-year students will take four or five classes each semester, usually grouped into Monday/Wednesday/Friday (MWF) or Tuesday/Thursday (TTh) time slots, so that your first semester schedule will probably look something like this:

	MONDAY	TUESDAY	WEDNESDAY	THURSDAY	FRIDAY
8 am	English	Spanish	English	Spanish	English
9 am	History	Art	History	Art	History
10 am					
11 am	Biology		Biology		Biology
12 pm					
1 pm					
2 pm					
3 pm					
4 pm					
5 pm					
6 pm					
7 pm					
8 pm					
9 pm					
10 pm					
11 pm					

Isn't that amazing? When I got my first semester schedule, I thought this college thing was going to be a breeze compared to high school. I could finish by lunch every day and have the rest of my time to do as I pleased.

But wait. What about science lab, sports practice, and your work-study job in the cafeteria? Did you remember study time? The average college class will require two hours of prep for each hour in class. If you're taking fifteen hours of class each week, that's thirty hours of studying. And, you do have to eat. Let's figure all that in now:

	MONDAY	TUESDAY	WEDNESDAY	THURSDAY	FRIDAY
8 am	English	Spanish	English	Spanish	English
9 am	History	Art	History	Art	History
10 am	Study	Art	Study	Art	Study
11 am	Biology	Study	Biology	Study	Biology
12 pm	Lunch	Lunch	Lunch	Lunch	Lunch
1 pm	Study	Biology Lab	Study	Biology Lab	Study
2 pm	Study		Study		Study
3 pm	Study	Study	Study	Study	Study
4 pm	Sports Practice	Sports Practice	Sports Practice	Sports Practice	Sports Practice
5 pm	Sports Practice	Sports Practice	Sports Practice	Sports Practice	Sports Practice
6 pm	Dinner	Dinner	Dinner	Dinner	Dinner
7 pm	Cafeteria Job	Cafeteria Job	Cafeteria Job	Cafeteria Job	Cafeteria Job
8 pm	Cafeteria Job	Cafeteria Job	Cafeteria Job	Cafeteria Job	Cafeteria Job
9 pm	Study	Study	Study	Study	
10 pm	Study	Study	Study	Study	
11 pm	Study	Study	Study	Study	

Oh my. Where did all that free time go? And, I didn't even include student club meetings or conferences with professors. Of course, you could try to squeeze all your studying into the weekends, but it won't work. You can probably prepare for your Monday classes on Sunday, but your Spanish exercises for Thursday can't be done until Tuesday since you wouldn't have covered those verb tenses yet, and you won't even know the topic for your short history paper (due Friday) until Wednesday morning. In any case, weekends are often filled with working to pay the tuition bill. I don't mean to make it look impossible, since not all classes will require the same amount of work. Also, some weeks of the semester will require less work than others, but there will also be weeks when you'll be pulling three all-nighters just to finish your research projects.

I'll talk about the crucial issue of time management later, but the moral of this story is that college allows you more flexibility than high school did, but requires much more time.

CLASSES

First of all, you don't have to raise your hand and ask permission to use the restroom. Just get up quietly and go if you need to.

But more important, college classes are much harder than high school. You will cover roughly twice as much material in the same amount of time. In addition, as we saw earlier, you only meet two or three times each week instead of every day. You can do the math and see that in order to cover so much material in so little time, you will be moving at a blistering pace. As soon as you've finished non-truth-functional connectives in logic class, you'll be covering indeterminacy and quantificational equivalence before you can even catch your breath.

This brings us to an important point—*never fall behind in class*. In high school maybe you could miss a few days or not complete the readings and still understand most of what was going on. In college, your classmates will have moved on to the age of Pericles while you're still trying to figure out who won the Battle of Thermopylae.

Finally, in college there's no such thing as doing your work in class. I remember in my high school courses, our teachers would often explain a concept for the first part of the hour, then give us time to work at our desks on assignments. In college, all your time is spent listening to lectures or discussing a text. There's no such thing as having free time before the bell rings.

TEACHERS

High school teachers should have their salaries doubled—or at least get more breaks during the day. I have never known a group of people who work harder and put up with so many difficulties to get the job done. Not only do they teach at least twice as many hours each week as your average college professor, they usually get paid less and have to pull shifts as lunchroom monitors or prom chaperones. And, needless to say, there are plenty of times they are not given the respect they deserve by students or parents.

College professors, on the other hand, do not have to put up with many discipline problems. I can count on one hand the times I've had to ask a student to stop talking in class. Since they are all adults and are paying a lot amount of money to be there, students usually behave themselves and pay attention in college classrooms. After all, everyone is an adult—if you don't want to be in a class, you simply drop it.

You have to realize that college professors will not coddle you. If you miss a reading or paper assignment because you're absent one day, the professor will expect you to find out what it was before the next class. If you are sick, it is your job, not the professor's, to work out a way to make up your assignments. The burden of responsibility in college is on you. As I said, you're a grownup now.

TYPES OF
PROFESSORS

Professors come in as many varieties as breakfast cereals, but there are some important distinctions and common types within the profession that can help you better understand who you're working with (or what you're up against).

TENURE-TRACK
VERSUS ADJUNCT

In the ivy-covered world of academe, the Holy Grail for professors is tenure. Tenure is a lifetime guarantee of employment, an almost unbreakable job contract that assures professors cannot be fired or lose their jobs at their college or university except under the most extraordinary of circumstances—such as if the school goes bankrupt or they beat up a student in front of an entire class (and even then it's not always a sure thing). Tenure was originally designed to protect professors with unpopular opinions from arbitrary dismissal by angry college officials. While this is still true, today it is more of a reward for loyal service. The tenure process for a new professor usually takes six or seven years, during which time young professors work very hard to be good teachers, write respected articles or books, and meet the expectations of their senior colleagues. More often than not the process is smooth, but everyone in the field knows countless stories of brilliant teachers and researchers who were torpedoed by some cantankerous old grump in their departments or because they accidentally totaled the dean's car on the way to the grocery store.

Adjunct professors, on the other hand, are hired on a yearly or course-by-course basis. They have no hope of tenure and rarely any long-term prospects of employment. They are usually poorly paid, receive few if any benefits such as health insurance, and are treated by most of their tenure-track colleagues with polite indifference at best. Many adjuncts teach at more than one college, driving many miles a day between schools just to make ends meet. Adjunct professors are particularly numerous at state schools and two-year colleges, but many of the most prestigious universities in the country employ more adjuncts than they will ever admit to on a campus tour.

Why should you care about any of this? In most cases you shouldn't, since American History or Abnormal Psychology are basically the same courses whoever teaches them. However, continuity is the big issue for students. A tenure-track, and especially, a tenured professor is far more likely to be around next year to teach your favorite course or write a recommendation for you than an adjunct professor. Does this mean you should avoid adjuncts? Absolutely not. I'll let you in on a little secret—adjunct professors are often the best teachers at a college. Their sole job is to instruct. They don't have to write books, serve on tedious college committees, or worry about earning tenure. And, considering the conditions they have to put up with, few adjuncts would take on the job unless they genuinely loved teaching. Just remember, if an adjunct professor is scheduled to teach a course you want or need next semester, sign up now. And, if you need recommendation letters from your favorite adjunct professors, get them before the end of the year. You never know if they'll be back.

LECTURER / ASSISTANT / ASSOCIATE / FULL

Professors have ranks, just like the military. At the bottom are lecturers—usually adjunct professors who are hired on a temporary basis. Next come assistant professors, the lowest rung of the tenure-track ladder. If an assistant gains tenure, she is then promoted to associate professor and is considered a senior faculty member. After a number of years, if an associate professor serves the college well or becomes a leader in her field, she can be promoted to full professor. A particularly distinguished or well-connected senior professor can also be offered an endowed chair—usually named after a big donor—which doesn't necessarily mean much except that she has a longer title on her business card.

Again, these ranks are not particularly important to students no matter how much professors themselves may obsess over them. The only thing you need to be aware of is that senior professors are more experienced—but not necessarily better—teachers. They usually know their material well and can handle just about any question you might throw at them. But there are a few senior professors out there who mentally retired the day after they earned tenure. They lecture in a dull monotone from the same yellowing notes they used during the Nixon administration. Younger professors, on the other hand, though sometimes lacking in experience, often make up for it in energy and familiarity with the latest trends in the field. If you're anxious to hear the most recent news on literary theory or genetics, take a course from an assistant professor.

GRADUATE ASSISTANTS

One of the primary missions of large private and public universities is to train the next generation of professors. Students in graduate programs at these schools are usually required to serve as apprentices to established professors, just as medical students work with experienced physicians. Often this means grad students will teach small, weekly meetings of a professor's large lecture course. Sometimes they will act as tutors in a seminar, supervise a lab section, or teach freshman composition. Graduate assistants are rare at liberal arts colleges, but if you attend a larger university, you will almost certainly have them as teachers.

Never underestimate the power of graduate assistants. Even though they don't have titles in front of their names, they can make or break your grade in a course. Professors usually let grad students determine the final grades for their particular sections—only in extreme circumstances will a professor step in to overrule a graduate assistant's decision. If you go over the head of your graduate assistant by appealing to the professor, you will need a very good reason.

Even though grad students are new to their subjects, they are usually eager to do a first-rate job in their courses. They work hard preparing classes on top of their own heavy workloads. They often keep the same nocturnal hours as undergraduates, so meeting you for a late-night review session is no big deal for most. They even know the latest movies and will understand contemporary cultural references that leave older professors scratching their heads. In addition, graduate students can write helpful recommendation letters. You'll want most references to be from professors, but an additional letter from a graduate assistant familiar with your work is icing on the cake.

THE DEPARTMENT CHAIR

Every department of a college or university has a chair in charge of professors, students, staff, budgets, curriculum, and relations with the central administration. They are almost always senior professors with years of experience in their fields and great familiarity with the inner workings of their own schools. You may have a department chair as a teacher in a course, but you won't notice any difference when he stands in front of your class.

A department chair becomes important to a student in those, fortunately, rare cases when a student can't work out a problem with a professor. If your professor never shows up for class, grades your papers in a patently unfair manner, or delights in publicly humiliating you, the department chair for that course is the one you should see. But as before, be certain you have a solid case before you take this step.

If you get to know a chair as one of your professors, be
sure to ask her to write one of your recommendation letters.
Chairs are not usually better professors than anyone else in
their departments—often they take the job because no one
else wants it—but there's a certain panache about having
Chair, Department of Biomedical Engineering under their signa-
tures that may impress potential employers or graduate admission committees.

Now that we've covered the official divisions among professorial ranks, let's look at some common types of college teachers. No real-life professor perfectly fits into this field guide, of
course, but I think you'll recognize a few of your current or
future professors in the examples that follow.

THE STAR

Usually found in ivy league universities, star professors are internationally known as authorities in their subjects. The university has paid big bucks to recruit these luminaries and features them prominently in mailings to high school seniors, graduation ceremonies, and alumni magazines. You may have been drawn to a university for the opportunity of studying at the feet of these shining stars. Good luck. Their courses— which they usually teach on a less frequent basis than normal professors—are often booked a year in advance and reserved only for a few select majors or graduate students. If you do manage to get into one of their classes, they will frequently be away on lecture tour or in Stockholm accepting their latest Nobel Prize. Stars are usually very nice people, if you can get to know them, and many are excellent teachers, but undergraduate instruction is rarely their focus. If you get the chance, do take a class from them, but don't expect the same attention you would get from your other professors.

THE ECCENTRIC GENIUS

You already know this type from childhood movies. They have a wild mane of hair, no social skills, and often get lost wandering the halls of their own departments. But, they are brilliant researchers who have discovered a cure for the common cold or deciphered a mysterious language that has baffled scholars for generations. Most campuses have a few geniuses locked away somewhere deep in a lab or library. The trick is to find them. They rarely show up for departmental receptions—and when they do, they stand in a corner staring at their shoes. If professors in general are shy, geniuses are doubly shy. Students often fall asleep in their classes since few are dynamic teachers. But, if you have the opportunity to get to know a genius, jump at it.

You have to proceed slowly and cautiously so you don't frighten them away. Mention after class that you read their articles in the latest journals and were hoping you could ask a question. Sign up for more than one of their courses so they can get to know you better. If the chance arises, offer to be their research assistant. You won't meet many genuine geniuses after you graduate from college, so take advantage of the situation while you can.

THE RADICAL

Professors are generally more politically active than the average population group. This is understandable when you consider most of them are smart, disciplined individuals who could have made it big in the corporate world if they had wanted to. Instead, they are idealists who gave up a large salary so they could pursue their dreams of academic life. Most professors are politically liberal or moderate, but whatever their affiliation, there are always a few professors on campus who are vividly outspoken and pride themselves on their activism. No student in any of their courses ever escapes without hearing their views on gun control, religion, capital punishment, euthanasia, free trade, or whatever their cause might be.

Let me state my own prejudice here—I like political activists. I respect anyone on either side of an issue who thoughtfully engages with a problem and advocates workable solutions. I think professors should be as deeply involved as they wish in local, state, national, and international issues. I just don't think they should bring their views into the classroom. No student paying hard-earned money to attend college should be forced to listen to professors expounding personal views on controversial issues, especially if they are only tangential to the subject of the course. Granted, if a professor is teaching a course on the environmental history of the Amazon basin, it's going to be hard to avoid discussing the foolishness of clear-cutting rain forests. But, most issues have at least two sides that thoughtful people of good conscience have embraced. A professor should always strive to present these issues clearly in an unbiased way.

When a professor's personal views start affecting student grades, then things become inexcusable. I have talked with too many students who have told me the same story. They are taking a course from Professor X and have just gotten back their first paper. They took an opposite view on a issue from that argued in class by the professor and received a C or worse on the paper, while another student who followed the party line earned an A. Both papers were of similar length and quality, but the student who parroted back the professor's view received the better grade. Believe me—it happens. Professors will always tell you in class they respect those students who disagree with them as long as they make a good argument. Most of them truly do and will fairly grade a paper or test that takes a stand opposite their own. But, there are some who won't, no matter what they may say behind the lectern. Students placed in this horrible situation have two choices— they can stand their ground and earn a poor grade or they can give the professor what they want and watch their GPA rise. You can try talking with the professor, but most would be shocked—shocked—that you would think them prejudiced graders, and you'll only make things worse in the end. I can't state the best course of action for you except to drop the course if you still can. If you can't, you have a tough choice to make.

THE INCOMPREHENSIBLE LECTURER

I grew up in San Antonio and did my undergraduate work at the University of Texas. While I was there, I had a professor in a large astronomy lecture course who was born and raised in Boston. I couldn't understand a word he was saying—or at least I had a lot of trouble. He was an excellent and engaging speaker, but it took me several minutes to figure out that a "stah" was a bright object shining in space.

No matter where you grew up, in college you are going to have professors who have very different accents from your own. Even professors from your own hometown are sometimes poor speakers. In either case, you will not be getting the crucial information you need to do well in a course. But I can suggest several strategies.

DID YOU KNOW?
Most college professors get paid vacations called sabbaticals. Every few years (seven is average), professors can apply to have a semester or even a full year off to finish a book or brush up on their Swahili. This is great for professors, but it can cause havoc for students needing a course offered only by the absent faculty member.

First, try moving to the front of the class. You will, of course, hear the professor better, but you can also see him speak. Body language can be surprisingly helpful in understanding difficult speakers. And if that doesn't work, try the opposite—close your eyes and listen. This forces you to focus on the professor's words rather than distracting external factors (such as the person in the row in front of you). Third option— go to their office hours for clarification. Don't say, "Professor Smith, I need to clear some things up because you mumbled incoherently to the blackboard during our last class." Instead, just ask if you could go over a few points of the lecture you didn't quite understand. If none of these strategies work and there is another section still open, switch to it immediately.

THE DEN MOTHER

These professors bake chocolate chip cookies for their students during finals week, show up for college softball games to cheer on the team, and always have a sympathetic ear for student problems. You might be tempted to confuse such a professor with your dear Aunt Edna or Uncle Joe, but that would be a mistake. Den Mothers can be as hard as nails if you persistently turn in late papers or sleep through exams. If you have one for a teacher, never try to take advantage of his or her kindness.

THE STEADY TROOPER

Most professors fall into this category. They are neither saints nor sinners, just hard-working teachers trying to do their best for their students. Their basement may have flooded that morning or their son may have just dropped out of Princeton to join a cult, but they still show up for classes and do their jobs. They faithfully teach courses, grade papers, advise students, serve on college committees, and coach the neighborhood soccer team. They make more than parking lot attendants, but not nearly as much as if they'd gone to medical school like their mothers wanted. But, they love their jobs and wouldn't trade them for the world.

COLLEGES AND PROFESSORS

It is not just individual personalities that play a role in what your professors will be like. The type of higher education institution you attend can make a huge difference in what your experiences with professors will be. You will find all manner of teachers at every college, but there are certain qualities—call them environmental factors—that go along with most professors at each type of school. Knowing these can give you a big advantage whether you're attending a distant university or your local community college.

MAJOR RESEARCH UNIVERSITIES

A research university can be private or public, but one quality they all have in common is that their professors are expected to be on the cutting edge of scholarship in their fields, whether it be nanotechnology or post-modern poetry. Most ivy league schools, major state universities, and just about any large, famous school you can think of will fall into this category. They have huge amounts of money available to lure both top professors and the most promising students from around the world. Earning a degree from one of these schools can often be a ticket to a great job or top graduate school. Research universities also offer students tremendous resources, like the latest scientific equipment, vast libraries with all the latest books and journals, and access to some of the best minds in academics.

Some of the most dynamic and caring teachers in the world work at top research universities. They will bend over

---

QUICK TIP

If you want to strike up a conversation with a college professor but don't know what to say, ask about his or her specialty. Everyone with a PhD has spent years researching some tiny area of human knowledge until they know more about it than just about anyone else on the planet. Professors like to talk about what's important to them—and you just might learn something interesting.

backward to share their time and expertise with undergraduates. But here's the problem—at research universities, professors are under tremendous pressure to publish or perish. In matters of tenure and promotion, they are judged on the quantity and quality of their books and academic articles as much as they are on teaching. They will therefore be grateful if you respect their time constraints and visit them during scheduled office hours rather than just dropping by for a chat.

LARGE STATE UNIVERSITIES

Megaschools with fifty thousand students usually fall under the research university category as well, but they have a few special characteristics all their own. Classes at these schools are often so large that the professor is little more than a distant figure at the front of an enormous lecture hall. This is especially true with first-year courses. In fact, your entire freshman year can go by in such universities without ever having a conversation with a professor. Again, it's not that the professors in these schools enjoy the lack of contact with students, but because of budget constraints and the sheer number of students attending the university, departments are forced to have enormous classes.

But there are ways to get more out of such courses. After every lecture, you'll see a small group of students gathered around the professor asking questions or just talking. Join this group. Even if there are five hundred people in the class, it's a guaranteed way for you to talk one-on-one with the professor on a regular basis. Ask a question from the readings or request a clarification about some point in the lecture. I know, back in high school such people were considered overeager boot lickers, but it's time to move on. If you want to be more than just a number, you're going to have to work at it.

I'll also let you in on one of the best-kept secrets at large state universities—the honors program. Almost every major university has a small honors house tucked away in some corner of the campus. These programs are absolute gems because they attract the best teachers and students from the whole school. Instead of being lost in a class of hundreds, students in these programs meet with just a dozen or so classmates around a seminar table. Professors actually fight to teach honors classes—and why wouldn't they? Instead of lecturing to a vast herd of students they'll never get to know, they have the opportunity to work closely with the brightest young minds at the university. If you're a high school senior heading for a large university or a first-year college student already there— and if you're grades are good—find out about the honors program. Admission to these programs is usually competitive, but if you can get in, you'll have the best of both worlds—a chance to work closely with great professors while paying low tuition.

Since such programs often have their own social life, you'll also have frequent opportunities to get to know your fellow honors students and professors outside the classroom.

COMMUNITY COLLEGES

Local two-year colleges have long been underappreciated, but they are one of the best deals in higher education. For a fraction of the cost of going away to school, you can attend the same classes you would find at four-year schools. For people who have financial, family, or other restrictions that make staying near home advantageous, community colleges are a great alternative. At the end of two years, you can then take your credits and transfer to a four-year college to complete your degree.

In spite of the good things community colleges have going for them, there are some drawbacks, especially regarding professors. A large percentage of teachers at community colleges are adjunct instructors who have full-time jobs elsewhere. Naturally enough, they are not going to be hanging around campus very much (many don't even have offices), so you have to schedule meeting times around their busy schedules. Very often, they don't know if they'll be there from semester to semester, so developing long-term relationships with them can also be a challenge.

Some of the best professors in the country teach at community colleges. They don't have to worry about publishing, so they can devote their attention solely to their students. They're not in it just for the money (the salaries are usually low) or the prestige, but because they like teaching.

LIBERAL ARTS COLLEGES

Liberal arts colleges are one of the greatest inventions in higher education. They usually are made up of a couple of thousand bright students gathered together to learn from professors who know their subjects well and are devoted to teaching. There are many varieties of liberal arts schools—religious, secular, single-gender—but teaching is central at all of them. Even at the most prestigious liberal arts colleges, professors will not last very long unless they're committed to their students. The dean isn't going to care that they just won the Pulitzer Prize if they're failures in the classroom.

If liberal arts colleges are so great, why doesn't everyone attend them? Several reasons. First, they cost a lot of money. You can go to a nearby state school for about half the amount you'll spend at a liberal arts college. Second, not everyone likes small schools. If you went to a tiny high school, you may long for a university with unlimited course offerings, nationally known sports programs, and every imaginable student activity. Third, liberal arts colleges are very often in the middle of nowhere. If endless miles of cornfields or a lack of good ethnic restaurants doesn't appeal to you, you might be pretty miserable for four years.

But, in return for these drawbacks, you'll get some of the most devoted teachers you can imagine. Liberal arts professors still write important books and are leaders in their fields, but teaching is their focus. They'll have time for you when you need extra help or want to talk about your future plans. They're not perfect, but liberal arts professors know that college is ultimately about the students.

TRANSFERRING

There are many good reasons for changing colleges, but there are just as many bad ones. Some students find out too late that their chosen school doesn't have a particular program they're interested in, like Arabic or physical therapy. Other students find that there is too much or too little social life at their college. Sometimes a student realizes that picking her father's alma mater was a big mistake even though Dad was so proud when she was admitted. In such cases, transferring to a different college or university may be a very good idea. After all, you are making a huge investment of time and money in whatever school you attend, so it had better be one that works for you.

But, I have also known many students who transfer for the wrong reasons. One bright young woman came to my office in tears a few years ago saying that college was miserable for her. She was fighting with her roommate, failing her classes, and missing her family terribly. She wanted to transfer to a college in her hometown and move back into her parents' house. I handed her a tissue and said that living in the room she had grown up in and attending school locally might be the right move for her, but I asked her to consider that the grass may not be greener elsewhere. Colleges have ways of helping you deal with roommate troubles, either by mediating conflicts or setting you up in a new place to live. Calculus and chemistry are just as hard at other schools, and moving back in with your folks may not be as much fun as you think. I advised her to work with the student-life office on roommate troubles, make an appointment with the academic support center to learn better study skills, and get involved with a group or two on campus so that she would feel more connected to the college and have more friends. It took a little time, but eventually she had a new roommate, was earning good grades, and was having fun on weekends instead of feeling homesick. It's not the answer for everyone, however if you find yourself in a similar situation, I'd bet your college has plenty of people to help you find happiness where you are.

If you do transfer to a different school, make sure that your class credits will go with you. Most of your courses will have equivalents at your new college, but it is quite possible that some classes will not transfer. Talk to the registrar's office at your target school before you sign any papers, and find out exactly which courses will count towards their requirements. Many transfer students end up taking extra classes or even an extra semester of courses to make their new program work.

I don't want to discourage anyone from transferring to a new college if it's the right move. I changed schools myself after my first year, and it was one of the best moves I ever made. But, remember what the Roman poet Horace said:

Sometimes when you sail across the sea,
all you really change is the sky above your head.

HOW TO FIND THE
BEST TEACHERS

Students often ask me whether or not a professor in some course they want to take is a good teacher. I'm usually not very helpful because, first, I've never taken a course from that professor and, second, even if I had something intelligent to say about the teaching skills of other faculty members at my college, I'm not foolish enough to criticize a colleague in front of a student. So, where do you go to get the inside scoop on which professors to take and which to avoid? There are several methods available for finding out how a professor is as a teacher, though each has its limitations.

But, first a cautionary word—*good* does not mean *easy*. Those professors who make you sweat in college are often the ones you learn the most from. Granted, there are times when you just want to find the smoothest way out of a course requirement, but a blow-off course where you barely crack a book to get a B+ will probably bore you to tears. On the other hand, there are professors out there who will work you to death and give you a poor grade anyway. So try this strategy—look for teachers who know their subjects, are good in the classroom, and are fair to students, even if they make you do problem sets every night.

TEACHING EVALUATIONS

At the end of every semester in college, you have to fill out evaluation forms for each course. Though many students see this as a hassle, it can be a very valuable tool for both teachers and students. Professors can read these anonymous evaluations to find out ways to improve their teaching. Administrators read them and see if they should hire the teacher again next term. Students can profit from them by getting hard data on what a particular professor is like.

Students don't actually get to read the evaluations themselves, but they can usually see a professor's scores on areas such as whether or not students think they grade fairly and return papers in a timely fashion. Most of the time, these results are available in a booklet or online. If your college doesn't automatically give you one each semester, ask for a copy at the dean's office or library.

It doesn't really matter if the particular course you're looking for is reviewed or not, because it's information on the professor, not the course, that you need the most. If the review covers a Hinduism class taught last year, but you want to know how that professor is in a Buddhism seminar, you can pretty well bet the experience in the two courses will be similar. All professors have their own styles, and they don't change that much according to what classes they're teaching. If their Shakespeare course is one dull lecture after another, their Milton class probably will be too. On the other hand, if they inspire their students in calculus, they will in differential equations as well.

WEBSITES

The last few years have seen the birth of websites devoted to giving the inside scoop on professors by allowing students to register their own classroom experiences for all the world to read. This kind of information is both very good and very bad. It's good because you can read in detail the first-hand experiences of students with professors. You can pick up great tips, such as "Professor Jones always gives easy multiple-choice exams," or "Don't take this course—you actually have to do the readings!"

However, these forums suffer from the same weakness as any other anonymous ranking system—there's no way to make sure the opinions offered are accurate or representative. All it takes to smear a professor is a small group (or even a single student with too much time on his hands) who got bad grades in the course. They can log on and write a dozen negative reviews over pizza at the campus grill. Of course, the opposite is also true. Even bad professors have their fans who can paint a rosy, but misleading, picture of a teacher's classroom performance. Bottom line—read the comments posted on these websites all you want, but never take them at face value.

ADD / DROP PERIOD

In most colleges, you have at least a couple of weeks to try out a course before you commit to it. Up until this magic date (noted on the official school calendar), you can sit in on a course, then drop it if you find it—or the professor—is just not for you.

QUICK TIP
Published student evaluations only give you a professor's ratings from the previous academic year. If professors are new or were on sabbatical last year or were sick the day evaluations were handed out, you won't be able to get any information about them.

This shopping period is one of the best ways possible for you to get an idea of what a professor is really like. But don't base your decision just on the first class meeting. Very often the first class is filled with administrative details, such as going over the syllabus, that don't give you much of a handle on how the class itself will be run. So, always go at least twice before you make any firm decisions.

There are, however, a few problems with shopping for classes like this. First, many professors don't give their initial test until several weeks into the course. You could be enchanted with a professor's spellbinding lectures and sparkling wit for over a month before the axe falls with the first exam.

The second danger with this method is the stuff of college nightmares. Many students will sign up for one or two more courses than they intend to take each semester with the idea of dropping the unwanted classes in the first couple of weeks.

DID YOU KNOW?

Students are often afraid to drop a class after the initial deadline because they will have a W (for *Withdraw*) on their transcripts. Fear not—you don't want three or four each semester on your permanent record, but an occasional W during college is not going to make any difference to employers or graduate schools.

This can be a good plan, since registering for a class assures you a seat in the course. So you shop classes for a week, then drop a couple and get a refund on your books. No problem— except on those occasions when you forget to officially drop the course. You meant to, but between swim team practice and a busted computer, you never actually filled out the form. Now it's two weeks before the end of the semester and you get a note from the dean reporting that you are failing a course you forgot about months ago. You rush to the professor for help, but he says he has no power to remove you from the course role after the drop date. You frantically try the registrar's office, but they say it's out of their hands. To make matters worse, the college is charging you extra tuition for the class you are going to get an F in. There are, sometimes, ways out of this horrible situation, but it will be more trouble than you can imagine. The moral of the story is, of course, don't let this happen to you. If you stop attending a course, make absolutely, positively sure that you are out.

OFFICE VISIT

There is a simple but often overlooked method for deciding whether or not you want to take a course from any professors talk with them. All you have to do is find out when their office hours are by looking at their doors or websites, then drop in for a short visit. Say that you're thinking about taking their courses, but just wanted to get a little more information on what will be covered, what the writing requirements are, etc. Of course, you want to know all these things, but what you're most after is a sense of whether or not you can work well with this professor. Chances are if she is engaging and genuinely interested in you in her office, she will be in the classroom as well.

WORD OF MOUTH

The final method for finding the good professors is the most reliable of all—talk with students who have had a professor in the past to get an honest assessment of how they are as teachers. You'll find most students will be willing and even eager to share their thoughts on Professor Green's horrendous history class. Like battle-scarred veterans of combat, they will regale you with horror stories of endless readings and impossible midterms. "Don't take Green," they will plead, "Sign up for Jackson's section instead." And most of the time, they'll be right.

But as always, consider the source of any advice yet get. If you ask a student who blew off a class and received a D what they think of a professor, the response will usually be negative. On the other hand, if you ask some young Einstein if a math class is difficult, their answer probably won't be representative.

But, what if you're new at a college and don't know anyone

yet? If you live on campus, let me introduce you to your new best friend—your Resident Assistant (RA). These are upper-level students who live on your dorm floor and make sure you don't play your music too loud. But, they are also a goldmine of information on every aspect of college life, including professors. If they haven't had the particular course or professor you're curious about, they probably know someone who has.

THE ROTTEN APPLE

What happens if, in spite of your most diligent efforts, you find yourself stuck in a class with a horrible professor? And, for whatever reason—maybe because you absolutely have to have the class this semester—you can't drop it or postpone it. This falls into the category of what your parents called making the best of a bad situation. The same thing is going to happen to you from time to time after college, so consider this good practice.

My advice would be to narrow down exactly what the problem is with the teacher and deal with it as best you can. If they give incredibly difficult tests, form a study group or get help from someone who survived the course in the past. If they are sticklers for proper footnote formats on research papers, become an expert on the MLA style sheet. If they are just unbelievably boring, drink a double espresso before each class to stay awake.

GOOD RELATIONS

Professors are people just like everyone else, so common courtesy is a good guide for your relations with them. But, unlike your dry cleaner or the guy who bags groceries for you, professors have an amazing amount of power over your life. This means, of course, that you will want to work hard to stay on their good side—no easy task since a few professors during your college years will invariably be difficult to get along with. But consider it a small investment that can yield big rewards. Yes, good relations can help you earn better grades, but they can also help you when it comes to recommendations, summer internships, scholarship money, and a hundred other aspects of college life.

HOW TO ADDRESS
YOUR PROFESSORS

How you address your professors depends on many factors such as age, college culture, and, above all else, their own preference. Some teachers will ask you to call them by their first names, especially if they're relatively young themselves. They enjoy the informal atmosphere and feeling of camaraderie generated by having everyone in the class on the same level. Some colleges, in fact, pride themselves on having all their faculty and students on a first-name basis. But beware—one of the surest ways to tick off professors is to call them by their first names against their wishes. Most professors see themselves in a position of professional authority over their students that they earned by many years of advanced study. They no more want to be called *John* or *Maria* than does your average physician.

Some college teachers like to be called *Doctor,* but again you have to be careful. Not all of your professors will have earned a PhD or equivalent degree, especially in fields such as art, music, and education. A professor who has earned only a master's degree will not enjoy correcting you. Even those who have a doctoral degree can be uncomfortable with the title. Personally, every time someone calls me *Doctor* I feel like I should be scrubbing for surgery.

This is why the generic title of *Professor* is so useful. It fits every college teacher regardless of age or what degree they earned. It's perfectly appropriate for graduate teaching assistants and grey-haired emeritus professors alike. Make it your default form of address for your teachers and you won't go wrong.

GETTING IN TOUCH

On the first day of class, your professors will usually give you a syllabus with contact information. This will often include their email addresses, office phone numbers, and—depending on the teacher—their home phone numbers. It's important to use whatever means of contact the individual professor prefers. If you don't, you can end up neglected or worse.

Email is a favorite way of getting in touch with a professor. The great advantage it holds is that you can send a message to your teachers at 3 A.M. without waking them up. It also gives you a chance to reflect a bit on what you want to say so you can get it just right. Your professor can then look over the email and respond to it whenever he has a few minutes. The flexibility aspect of email makes it a convenient tool for everyone.

But of course there can be problems. Some older professors hate email and don't use it even if their email address is listed in the campus directory. You could be waiting weeks and never get a response from them. Also, college professors get an amazing amount of junk email for some inexplicable reason.

It's possible that your plea for an extension on your term paper could be accidentally discarded by your professor along with solicitations for cheap life insurance. This is especially true if you use a return email address other than your official college account.

Calling a professor's office is also a great way to get in touch. I especially recommend it in those cases when you have a problem that is serious and needs to be dealt with as quickly as possible. If the professor isn't there, just leave a message—but be sure to give a telephone number where you can be reached. Also give your full name. I've had students leave messages like "Hey, Professor, this is David. Please call me back as soon as you can." Of course, I have six Davids in my classes that semester, so I then have to figure out who left the mysterious message.

Even if professors give you their home phone numbers, be very careful about using them. Some professors genuinely won't mind that you call them on nights and weekends just to ask a question or chat about a course. But most college teachers have busy lives outside of the classroom and would prefer to keep school and home separate. Many professors also keep very different hours from their students. Just because you're awake at 2 A.M., don't assume your professors are too. If your professor has given you her home phone number and you have a problem that truly can't wait, go ahead and call. But unless it's an emergency, you're better off sending an email or waiting until she's in her office the next day.

Dropping by your professor's office is the most direct way to get in touch with a teacher. There's nothing like face-to-face contact for getting answers to your questions or quickly solving a problem, but there are potential problems. First, your professor may not be there. Most professors teach six to twelve class hours per week, so they could easily be on the other side of campus when you stop by. Even if they're not teaching, they could be in a department, faculty, or committee meeting (you

QUICK QUESTION

If professors only teach six to twelve hours each week, what do they do with the rest of their time?

Grade tests and papers, meet with their students, prepare for class, direct independent studies and research projects, meet with their advisees, attend faculty meetings, attend departmental meetings, attend committee meetings, attend more committee meetings, visit with prospective students, write recommendation letters, plan the next semester, fill out faculty surveys, attend professional conferences, read the latest journal articles and books in their field, and try to find a little time to do some research and writing.

wouldn't believe how many meetings faculty have) or at the library or cafeteria. So, dropping by is a hit or miss process that can waste a lot of your time. Second, even if your professor is in his office, he may not want to be disturbed. This doesn't mean he doesn't like you, just that he has to grade papers, prepare a lesson, or do a hundred other tasks on his agenda that day. There's an informal code at most colleges for gauging whether or not to knock on your professor's door. If an office door is propped wide open, it means please come in. If it's open just a crack, this indicates the professor is working hard on something, but doesn't mind talking for a little while if you have a pressing problem. A shut door usually means please don't bother me right now unless you have a true emergency. I've seen a few professors chew out students for bothering them when their doors are closed. Most teachers will not be this rude, but you never know.

OFFICE HOURS

Most professors keep regular office hours on campus—a kind of open house when students can drop in for any reason. These will be listed in your course syllabus and posted on their doors. During these times, you should feel free to stop by and chat even if their door is closed.

I was surprised when I first became a professor at how seldom students come to office hours. I assumed there would always be a line of students halfway down the hall anxious to discuss a reading with me or get some extra help with Latin verb conjugations. But the truth is professors usually sit alone in their offices waiting for someone to stop by.

If you do go to office hours during one of those rare times when there is a line—such as right before a major test—limit yourself to a few of your most pressing questions. Be sure to take advantage of those lulls between exams and papers just to drop by and talk with your professors.

ADVISING

The college you attend will have some sort of advising program for new students. Most, but not all, will involve professors. At one end of the spectrum are colleges that assign you a professor as an advisor before you ever set foot on campus. This person will then meet with you during orientation to help you select classes and keep in close touch with you for the rest of your college career, especially during the first year when many students are lost and overwhelmed. At the other end, are colleges that send you into the jungle without a guide. You may technically have an advisor at these colleges, but he's impossible to get in touch with or doesn't know the answers to your questions if you can find him. Some schools have given up entirely on using professors as advisors and instead send you to an advising center much like the customer service counter at your local department store

Since getting good advice at the start of your college years is so important, you have to learn to navigate through whatever system your college has. The best colleges will make this easy for you, but those that don't won't be sympathetic when you've signed up for all the wrong courses and have to take an extra year to finish your degree. In the end, it's your responsibility to make the right choices in college, no matter what advice you may or may not have gotten from an advisor.

GENERAL ADVISING VERSUS ADVISING ON MAJORS

Advising in college is divided into two systems—general undergraduate education and departmental majors. When you walk onto campus the first day, you will probably not know what you want to major in. Even if you do, you will still have common course requirements that everyone has to fulfill. Most schools will assign you a professor that you will meet with to plan a schedule and make sure you're taking the right classes your first semester.

Whenever you make a firm decision about a major, you'll then fill out a form (colleges love forms) and be assigned a professor from your department as a major advisor. Sometimes you'll still keep the old advisor as well, but in general your major advisor will take over the task of guiding you for the rest of your time in college.

BE PREPARED

Before you go in to see your advisor for the first time, make sure you have a basic understanding of your school's requirements. A typical college will require its undergraduates to complete a writing course plus a series of classes distributed across various disciplines, such as the humanities, social sciences, and natural sciences. Every school has a different balance of requirements, so learn yours by reading the appropriate section of the catalog.

If you are already sure what you want to major in, find out what that department recommends for its first-year students. In some departments, if you don't start a required sequence of courses your first year you will be left behind. Majors such as English or history usually allow a fair amount of flexibility to their students. However, if you're in engineering or architecture, your courses will be pretty well mapped out for you from day one.

It will be a great help at your first advising meeting if you know the basics of what your college requires and have selected possible courses for your semester. Always have two or three back-up courses in case your first choices are full. It also helps a lot to plot out a grid of when your desired courses meet during the day. You don't want to have more than two classes back-to-back if possible or your brain will be fried by your third class.

ADVISORS

Whether you're dealing with a general or major advisor, sometimes you will feel like you're totally on your own. A few professors see advising, particularly general undergraduate advising, as a chore best avoided whenever possible. To be fair, it is a tough job. I've had students come to me during orientation week with the most perplexing questions. A typical scenario:

Student: "Professor, I had two years of advanced AP chemistry at my high school and want to sign up for Organic Chemistry this fall, but I'm not sure if I need the lab this semester or next. What should I do?"

Me: "Um, well, I'm not sure—let me look at my advising handbook."

Literature professors are usually not the best people to ask about science requirements, nor do most biologists know how many years of Russian are needed before you can take advanced composition. If you give students the wrong answers, you can mess up their whole year and end up costing them lots of money.

Hence the most important rule of college advising: *Always verify anything your advisor tells you.* You can usually rely on advice from departments about their particular majors, but general undergraduate advisors can be more lost in the woods than you are. They may be trying their best, but you have too much at stake to sign up for the wrong courses. Check the catalog, ask your RA, double-check at the dean's office, but do whatever it takes to follow the official rules of your college.

Another little-known fact is that you can change advisors if you feel yours just isn't working out. If a friend tells you she has a great advisor and yours is miserable, go to your college administrative office and see if you can switch.

PLANNING YOUR COURSES

The particular courses you take in college are up to you and your advisor, but there are some general principles every student should follow:

- If your college requires a writing course, take it as soon as possible. Your school may make you do this anyway, but even if they don't you should sign up quickly—during your first semester if possible. Many of your college classes will require papers, so you want to have the necessary writing skills under your belt before you take these courses.

- If you have an opportunity to take a first-year seminar, jump at it. These courses give you a chance to work closely with a professor in a small-group setting. It's excellent preparation for later seminar work, and you develop a relationship with a professor at the beginning of your college career that can last for the next four years and beyond.

- Don't overload yourself your first semester. No matter how brilliant you were in high school, college is a whole new experience. You need time to adjust to lots of new pressures—so unless you're a certified genius, taking calculus, physics, chemistry, and three other courses all at the same time is going to break your spirit and your GPA.

- Remember that many classes have required labs or discussion sections. Usually you have to sign up for these separately, so don't forget to factor them into your schedule.

- If you have even a remote desire to study abroad in your junior or senior year, try very hard to complete all your basic college requirements before you go. You don't want to squeeze in leftover general education classes along with remaining courses for your major after you return. And, of course, if you want to study in a non-English-speaking country, develop your language skills as soon as possible.

- If you can afford it, consider signing up for a summer school class at your college *before* you begin in the fall. This will allow you to get a course or two behind you to lighten your load for the coming academic year. It also gives you a great chance to get comfortable with the school. You can then sit back and relax while all the other dazed students wander around campus in September.

HOW TO GET INTO A
CLOSED COURSE

One of the most frustrating experiences you'll have in college is getting shut out of a course you want or need. You might expect that $40,000 a year would buy your way into any course you'd like, but it doesn't work that way. This is especially common during your first year, when you're at the bottom of the pecking order for course registration. Seniors get to sign up first, then juniors, sophomores, and finally you. When it's your turn, the only open course left may be an 8 A.M. section of elementary woodworking.

There is, however, a secret method of getting into closed courses:

- Get on the waitlist immediately. You may be number five over the class limit of thirty, but you'll at least be ahead of the twentieth person on the waitlist. As people drop the course, you'll move up the waitlist ladder and may get into the course automatically after a few days.

- Contact the professor teaching the class, preferably in person. Express to her your burning desire to learn about medieval Japanese history, music theory, or whatever the subject might be. Don't lay it on too thick, but a sincere interest can open doors.

- If you are a major in that department or even thinking about becoming a one, let the professor know. Departments usually go the extra mile to help out their own.

- Buy the books and attend the class. Sit close to the front with a smile on your face and diligently take notes. If you get into the class, you'll need the information anyway. If it's still up in the air, your obvious interest may move the professor to let you in.

- If, after a week or so, the professor still says there's no way you can get in the class, say thank you, remove yourself from the waitlist, and get a refund on your books. It could be that the professor truly can't raise the limit without angering the department chair or that he simply doesn't want a larger class. You can always try again next year when your sophomore status will let you register earlier.

CHOOSING A MAJOR

I won't presume to advise you on what you should major in at college, but I would like to offer one word of wisdom based on years as a professor and advisor— *relax*. Most of my former students are in successful careers that are only vaguely related to their college major. Art majors go to medical school, chemistry students become investment bankers, and law school—well, you can major in anything and still go to law school.

The most important lessons college will teach you are how to write well, think critically, organize your time, and play well with others. You will learn these skills no matter what you major in. It's very likely that your career will change more than once after graduation anyway, so narrow preparation in our ever-changing economy can end up backfiring on you. I'm not saying you shouldn't be practical—combine a minor in business with your dance major, if it would make you and your parents more comfortable, but the best advice in the end for choosing a major is to follow your heart.

QUICK TIP

If you really need help, talk to a departmental secretary. Professors are great for questions about their courses or areas of expertise, but they rarely know much about important paperwork or the essential details of a department.

THE CLASSROOM

The average college classroom is more like a wrestling arena than a movie theater. It's a place where you need to actively engage with your professors and the constantly new ideas they're presenting to you. If you just sit back and wait passively to be taught, you might as well be munching popcorn down at the local cineplex.

Classrooms come in all shapes and sizes, from enormous lecture halls seating hundreds to small seminar rooms. For every sort, there are important strategies concerning what to do and not to do if you want to get good grades and impress your professors.

WHERE TO SIT

In large lecture rooms, you want to find a seat that gives you a good view of the front of the class and places you in the professor's line of sight. You might think the front row would be the best place, but it isn't. Try this experiment—some time before class begins, when the room is empty, go up to the front of your lecture hall and stand behind the podium. Look out at all the seats and pretend you're lecturing to the entire class. Which seats do your eyes fall on most frequently? If you're like most people, you'll find yourself looking somewhere in the middle of the class. This is where professors usually focus their gaze and that's where you want to be. In a lecture hall of twenty rows, try sitting in about row four or five. This is close enough to see and hear well, but not so close that the professor is staring out over your head. Sitting on an aisle a few rows back is also good, since you don't blend into the crowd as much as in the middle. Never sit on the far side sections if you can help it. Most of us have terrible peripheral vision and will not see a raised hand over against the side wall unless you stand up and shout. The back row is also a mistake. Justified or not, professors assume anyone sitting that far away from them is a slacker trying to avoid attention.

The middle-front part of the classroom is also where you'll be able to best read all the material the professor puts on the board. Some teachers use the latest in digital technology, some still write on the board and make the chalk squeak (this is fun to do if you see people dozing off). Whatever the medium, you don't want to miss anything, so sit where you can clearly see everything.

The same rules hold, though not as strictly, for middle-sized rooms seating thirty to forty. Again, try for somewhere in the middle-front part of the class, even if you have to crawl over someone to get there. In small seminar rooms, it doesn't really matter where you sit, though consistently taking the seat next to the professor means you really have to be on your best behavior.

ASKING QUESTIONS

Professors like students who ask questions in class, as long as you do it correctly. In seminar classes you should generally feel free to ask a question or make a comment whenever there's a break in the conversation. You don't want to actually interrupt the professor, but most value back and forth dialogue in such courses.

In larger classes, especially lecture courses, you have to be more careful when you speak. As a general rule, the larger the class is, the less appropriate it is to freely ask questions. Some professors don't want to be interrupted at all during a lecture and will reserve time at the end for any questions or direct you to their office hours. Others will pause periodically to give students a chance to clarify something. Even if they don't announce their policy at the beginning of the semester, you'll quickly get a feel for a particular professor's own informal rules.

If you have professors who don't mind questions during lectures, do at least wait until they finish whatever thought they're on. Then follow the rules you learned back in elementary school—raise your hand, be polite, share time with others. At least once (probably more) in your college years, you'll have a class with a know-it-all student who takes up way more than her fair share of class time commenting on the subject of the day. Professors will usually discourage these folks early on as a service to the rest of the class, but some never get the message from their teachers or from peer pressure.

I know you've heard this a million times, but never be afraid to ask dumb questions. If you don't know something, chances are most of the class doesn't either. You are paying way

QUICK TIP

The world has never been kind to left-handed people (no coincidence the Latin word for "left" is *sinister*) and this extends to the college classroom. Most small and medium size classrooms will have only right-handed desks, but large lecture halls will often have a few left-handed seats scattered around the edges. If you're a leftie, get to class early and grab one before they're all gone.

too much money and investing far too much of your time in college to be afraid of asking any professor a question.

DISCUSSION SECTIONS

One of the hardest jobs many professors have is leading discussion sections for large lecture classes. In research universities this is often done by graduate students, but in smaller colleges full-time faculty fill the position. Typically, a lecture class will break into smaller groups once or twice a week. This gives you a chance to discuss the course material with a teacher and perhaps twenty other students in a way that's impossible in a lecture hall.

The reason these discussion sections are difficult for professors is that students are often reluctant to speak up in class. This may be because they're shy and afraid of embarrassing themselves in front of other students or maybe they just didn't do the readings for that week. Whatever the reason, pity the poor professor who poses question after question to such a group, just to meet blank stares and silent tongues. Leading a discussion section is definitely an art, but even the best teacher can have a class that makes him feel like a dentist pulling teeth.

So here's your chance to shine. If you can be one of those bright faces who always has something useful and intelligent to say in response to questions, your professor will love you for it. I don't mean that you should raise your hand every time and dominate the discussion, but if you can help your professor out by regularly speaking up in class, you can almost count on a higher grade. Such participation shows interest and preparation, so of course you'll score points. And in the end, you'll also learn a lot more.

CLASSROOM ETIQUETTE

Classrooms are designed so that you can see and hear the speaker at the front of the room. What always amazes me is that some very smart students don't realize the opposite is also true—your professors can see and often hear you wherever you sit, even in large lecture halls. I know I said that some seats naturally get more attention from the podium than others, but if something even the slightest bit annoying or distracting is going on in row thirty-two, it's going to quickly catch your professor's attention. Good attention—such as a thoughtful answer to a question posed in class—is desirable. Bad attention is something you definitely want to avoid.

Certain types of classroom behavior are always a mistake, while others depend on the individual professor. Students often rush from class to class and don't have time for a leisurely lunch, so they try to eat in class. Never do this, especially in a small course, since you're going to distract the professor and the students around you with noisy wrapping paper and the smell of pepperoni. If you are in a large lecture hall and are absolutely starving, I recommend discretely munching on a breakfast bar. But even this will bother some teachers, so be careful. Drinking is usually fine in any class as long as you don't make slurping noises.

Few things irritate a professor more than the shrill ring of a cell phone in the middle of a lecture—unless it's an even more distracting musical ring. Always turn off your phone before class. If you're expecting an emergency call, set your phone on vibrate, then get up and leave the classroom before you answer.

Try not to look bored in class. Restless sighing and glancing at your watch every five seconds will not earn you any points with a professor. I know that listening to some lectures is as exciting as watching paint dry, but try not to show it. Master the art of keeping an interested look on your face at all times. Mentally you may be planning your spring-break trip to Cancun, but teachers will think you're hanging on their every word. This will be very good practice for all the committee meetings you'll have to attend after college.

Falling asleep in class is a definite no-no. I know from my years of living in a dorm as a faculty house master that students routinely stay up most of the night, then jump out of bed for an 8 A.M. class. But, nodding off in a lecture is bad form and will bring out the mean side in a few professors. Some will embarrass you in front of the rest of the class by slamming a book on the table and asking if you'd like a pillow. Others will wake you up and lecture you like your parents on the importance of getting a good night's sleep. But even those teachers who let you sleep will notice and remember at grading time.

As bad as sleeping in class is, it's infinitely worse to peruse the Internet. We might forgive a dozing student ("The poor dear, he's worked so hard on my research paper"), but pulling out the sports page in class will send even the most gentle professorial souls into fits of apoplexy. It's extremely disrespectful, so never do it. If you're that bored with the lecture, just get up and leave.

QUICK TIP

Size does matter. The smaller the class, the better your professor can work with you as an individual. If you have a choice of class times, picking an early morning section will almost guarantee you a small-group experience.

TAKING NOTES

You can't possibly write down everything a professor says in class nor should you try. Those of us who teach, generally try to focus on the subject at hand, but we often go off on tangents. The trick for you is to recognize what is important—a task not as simple as you might think. Good professors often subtly work in background material and even personal stories to make the course material stick in their students' minds long after they've forgotten Avogadro's number or who shot President Garfield.

WRITE IT DOWN

The first and most important rule of note taking is: *If the professor writes it on the board, write it in your notes.* In whatever class and whatever subject, if a teacher takes the time to walk up to the board and write something on it, you better believe it's important. It doesn't matter if it seems trivial at the time or that the professor is engaging in some spur-of-the-moment thought. If something is on the board, there's a high probability it will show up on a test. Every campus has a story of some doddering old professor who spent half a history class answering an off-the-wall question by diagramming the workings of a medieval catapult on the board while most of the class stared out the window—only to have a major essay question about medieval catapults on the final exam.

FACTS VERSUS IDEAS

Different subjects require different note-taking techniques. You wouldn't approach statistics the same way you would philosophy. In most math, science, and foreign language classes, you are expected to memorize and then use information to solve problems or master a skill. Courses in the humanities emphasize comprehension and analysis of complex ideas. You'll still have plenty of material to memorize, but your professor will be primarily interested in how you use that information to cogently argue a point, not that you can regurgitate it on a test. In first-year Latin class, I expect students to memorize a long list of irregular verbs, but I'm not looking for their thoughts on whether or not the pluperfect subjunctive is a good idea. On the other hand, in classical mythology I want students to think about the deeper meanings of stories. Sure, they need to memorize the names of gods and their various functions, but more important, they need to take that information and consider how it relates to Greek society, gender roles, universal themes, etc., because those are the sorts of questions that will be on the exam. Your note taking needs to reflect the differing goals of different courses.

IT WAS A DARK AND STORMY NIGHT

Here's a practice exercise from a hypothetical discourse on British literature. The professor walks up to the podium at the beginning of class, adjusts his tie, and begins the lecture:

Mary Wollstonecraft Godwin was born in England in August of 1797 and was almost eighteen years old when she ran off to France with her married lover, the famous poet Percy Bysshe Shelley. Soon she was pregnant and returned to England, though the premature child of this illicit affair died only a few days after her birth. The couple then traveled back to the continent where, as Mary later relates, she began forming her famous novel, Frankenstein, as part of a ghost-story contest between Mary, Shelley, and their friend Lord Byron on the night of June

16th 1816 at the Villa Diodati near Geneva—a lovely spot by the way. I was there just last summer and tripped over a stone in the courtyard while gazing at the soaring mountains. The doctor had to put my foot in a cast and I hopped along on crutches for the rest of the trip. Anyway, Shelley's wife committed suicide later that year, which conveniently cleared the way for Mary and Shelley to legally marry.

This would be just a fraction of an hour-long lecture, but what should you write down from it and remember for the test? Unless your professor is a fanatic for dates (rare among English teachers), Mary's birth month of August isn't noteworthy, while the year 1797 is important only to give you a general setting of her formative years—a turbulent period of revolutions, war, and scientific discoveries in Europe. The fact that Mary was a teenager when she ran away with Shelley and wrote *Frankenstein* is important as it makes her one of the youngest writers of a major work of modern fiction, in addition to being one of the first well-known women authors. The death of her first-born child only a year before starting *Frankenstein* may have been a big influence on the genesis of the dark story, so it's definitely worth recording. The ghost-story contest is a vivid detail, so be sure to write it down. Your professor's medical woes seem like pointless rambling at first, but they make the book more real to students since the same soaring mountains that distracted him are a primary setting of the novel. The suicide of Shelley's first wife is mentioned quickly at the end, but it may have left a powerful guilt in Mary which affected the development of the *Frankenstein* story.

How do you get all this down in less than a minute? The professor isn't going to stop for you to catch up, so unless you're a professional stenographer you'll have to abbreviate. You learned this in high school, but in college things move at an even faster pace. So if I were a student in the class, I'd probably write something like the following:

- *Mary Godwin, born England (1797)*
- *18 to Europe with Shelley (married)*
- *Soon pregnant, baby dies*
- *Frankenstein starts as ghost-story contest near Geneva (1816)*
- *Prof broke foot there looking at mountains (clumsy)*
- *Shelley's first wife commits suicide, they marry (guilt?)*

Then I would work on my notes during lunch to fill in a few details while they're still fresh in my mind. This is crucial because, when the test comes a month later, you will have forgotten almost everything said in class unless you have it in writing.

LISTEN FOR CLUES

You'd be surprised how often professors will tell you in class exactly what will be on the test. Sometimes this is direct, other times it is more subtle. If a professor says something like, "You really should know this" or "This formula is important," you'd be crazy not to write it down and underline it in red. But those are the easy cases. For less obvious points that will probably show up on an exam, look for clues such as repetition and body language. If a teacher mentions something twice during a class, even if an hour apart, look for it on the next test. Also

QUICK TIP

Laptop computers are convenient for taking class notes, but they can be a problem. For one thing, the clicking keys can be terribly annoying to your professor and classmates. If you start to get bored, they can also tempt you to ignore the lecture by playing solitaire or checking your email. Old-fashioned pen and paper are often your best bet.

watch how they lecture. If they vary from their normal routine to sit on the edge of a table, grasp the lectern, or step away from their notes and address the class in a confidential tone, be sure to feature that material prominently in your notes.

Some professors, especially in large lecture courses, record their lectures so that students can watch them in the library or online. As a rule, you should always attend the live lectures and save the video for emergencies or review only. If you decide to skip your chemistry class and catch the lectures just on video, you'll miss out on many important things, but especially classroom clues that can highlight important points for your notes.

HOW TO READ
A BOOK

C ollege professors love to assign insane amounts of reading material for their classes. One reason for this is that we are passionate about our areas of expertise and want you to be exposed to as much as possible during a single course. We also suffer from academic myopia and tend to forget that you have three or four other courses with equally heavy loads.

You cannot possibly read with care every word you are assigned in a typical semester—so what do you do? The answer is to read different types of material in different ways. Some assignments you should read slowly and with great diligence, while others you need to survey rapidly, plucking out the essential facts and ideas from an endless sea of words. Exactly how to proceed depends a great deal on your particular professor, but the following should give you some general guidelines.

READING A DIFFICULT BOOK

You will be required to read some very tough books in college. Let's face it, if Aristotle's *Nichomachean Ethics* were easy, they'd be selling it at your local convenience store. You are paying mountains of money to your college to be challenged, so challenge you we will. But whether it's Aristotle or a book on economic history, there is a simple principle that can help you work through difficult texts.

When you were a little kid and your parents signed you up for swimming lessons, I'm going to bet the instructor didn't take you down to the deep end of the pool on the first day and toss you in. First you splashed around the kiddie pool, then you practiced sticking your head under water and blowing bubbles. After many lessons and a few tears, you finally were swimming all over the place with your friends. Just as you eased into swimming, so you should ease into a difficult book. Never begin a challenging text by simply starting at the first page.

If the book has a dust jacket or description on the back cover, begin by reading that. Get a feel for who the author is and what the book is about, then look at the table of contents.

This is a layout of the topics the book will cover and in what order. If the book has a short introduction, biographical sketch of the author, or comments from the editor, take a close look at these. Then check out any maps or glossary of terms and flag these pages for reference. Finally you're ready to begin—but don't start reading carefully yet. First, skim through the book in a leisurely manner, sampling passages here and there to get a general sense of the contents. If the text has summary headings at the beginning of chapters, these will be a great guide to what lies in store. Now that you have a clear sense of what the book is about, turn to the first page and begin to read.

LITERATURE

English and literature-in-translation classes vary widely in the scope of their readings, but they typically assign more pages than any other courses on campus. A class on European literature, for example, might begin with *Beowulf* and include Chaucer's *Canterbury Tales*, Cervantes' *Don Quixote*, Milton's *Paradise Lost*, Dostoevsky's *Crime and Punishment*, and throw in a few other epics for good measure.

Literature professors will actually expect you to read everything they assign. Frequently they will put passages on tests taken directly from the readings and ask you to comment at length on them. If you skipped that passage as you were skimming over *The Wife of Bath's Tale,* you can kiss your A goodbye. If you are in a literature class and want to get a decent grade, you'll need to devote whatever time is necessary to reading the works carefully. You'll quickly get a sense from class lectures what your individual professor thinks is important in literature, be it gender roles, historical setting, class conflict, or other areas. Whatever your professor's interest, I would advise you to read the whole assignment carefully before class, then re-read any passages that come up in lecture or discussion. Don't make the mistake of not doing the readings, then highlighting only passages discussed in class for study. Professors are onto this old trick and will deliberately include sections not dealt with in class on the exam.

Pay special attention to the slow and deliberate reading of poetry. Most poems need to be read two or three times to understand the beauty and intricacy of the verse:

> *From fairest creatures we desire increase,*
> *That thereby beauty's rose might never die,*
> *But as the riper should by time decease,*
> *His tender heir might bear his memory.*

And that's just the opening few lines of Shakespeare's first sonnet. If you try to cram all 154 of them (fourteen lines each, of course) into one night, you'll learn nothing and blow the test. Poetry is something to be savored, not rushed through.

SOCIAL AND NATURAL SCIENCES

Texts from disciplines like history, psychology, and botany can be a joy to read—or they can be painfully dull. If you've been assigned a good book or article, count yourself lucky, but if you find yourself wading through page after page of monotonous prose, try the following:

- Read the first paragraph of a chapter or paper very carefully. Scholars are trained to summarize their arguments at the beginning. Look for the thesis or main argument that they are going to make.

- Read the final paragraph carefully as well. Just in case their point was unclear at the start, they will usually summarize it again at the end.

- Now that you know what the reading is about, look at the middle. The supporting arguments of a reading will usually be grouped into headings or at least paragraphs. Make sure you know what they are, with an appropriate example or two taken from each part of the text.

- When you're finished, write a brief outline of the reading in your notes with the author's thesis and supporting evidence. Use this to study for the test.

FOREIGN LANGUAGES

Never—I repeat—never try to skim through a foreign language textbook, especially in first-year language courses. French has six different forms for the present tense of the verb *to be* (*je suis, tu es,* etc.) and the only way to learn them is by careful memorization. Students are often pleased by how short a chapter of a foreign language textbook is compared to their political science or literature books. The reason, my friends, is that they are densely packed with essential material.

The best approach to a language chapter is to carefully read through it once, then go back a second time and really take it apart. Underline important grammatical points in red, draw boxes around sample noun declensions and verbal conjugations, note key sentence examples, and make flashcards

---

QUICK TIP

There is no substitute for reading a piece of literature yourself. Summaries can only give you highlights of a text, while Hollywood, by necessity or design, changes a story drastically before it hits the big screen. If you want to fail your next test, watch the movie instead of reading the book.

from vocabulary lists to drill yourself in spare moments. By the time you finish an elementary language course, your textbook should look like your dog has chewed on it.

HOW TO FIND CHEAP TEXTBOOKS

I really shouldn't tell you this, but there are ways to save some serious money on college textbooks instead of buying them new at your school bookstore.

Before anything else, talk with or email your professors several weeks before the semester begins and find out exactly which books they require for the course. Armed with this list, you can start to work.

Some students will try to get by with alternate editions of a text, especially novels, but do this at your own peril. If the professor is using one edition of a book and you have another, you could be lost when it comes to reading assignments, lectures, and class discussions. You may also be unable to recognize passages on the exam if your text is a different translation (this happens frequently in my classes when someone borrows grandpa's edition of Homer's *Iliad*).

I recommend instead sticking with the particular edition a professor requires, but finding a way to get it more cheaply. You could try your college library, but there are usually limits on how long you can keep a book. If another student or faculty member recalls the text, you could be forced to give it up the night before the big exam.

Some college bookstores now rent textbooks, and this can be a great way to get your texts at a cheap price. If your school does this, get there early before all the books are gone. Unfortunately, renting is only cost-effective for bookstores if they can rent the book several years in a row. If they can't get the professor to agree to use the same text for the following years, it probably won't be available for you.

Used books, however, are a great way to go, whether you buy them online, from other students, or at your college bookstore. Unless they are literally falling apart or are marked up beyond recognition with the previous owner's comments and doodles, used books are a dream for college students. They

DID YOU KNOW?
Cutting-edge scholarship in most fields is not found in textbooks, but in articles from academic journals. The process of writing and producing a book can take years, but journals have a much faster turn-around time. If you want to know the latest word on any subject, look at the most recent editions of scholarly journals in your school's library.

cost much less than new and sometimes have useful notes if they come from an earlier class with the same professor.

If you are one of those people who loves the smell of fresh glue as you open a shiny new book for the first time, at least consider selling it back at the end of the semester. You won't get nearly as much as you'd like, but you might earn enough to help with book purchases next year. However, if there's any chance you may need the book in future courses or just want to keep one of your favorite texts forever, then please do. I still have my intro to philosophy book with pizza stains on the Descartes pages. It brings back wonderful memories every time I open it.

WRITING GREAT PAPERS

Learning to write well is the centerpiece of your college education. Consider for a moment that everyone who is pre-med has to take at least one semester of calculus if they want to have a prayer of getting into medical school. But next time you're at your physician's office, ask when she last used calculus in her practice. Odds are she never has. It's great mental training and it weeds out a lot of people I'd rather not have holding my life in their hands, but it's not a very practical skill for most doctors. The same goes for much of what you learn in college—but not writing. Whatever you do with your life, you will write.

Thanks to technology, writing has experienced a renaissance unequaled since Gutenberg invented the printing press. Electronic communication aside, almost every job you'll hold during your life will still require clear writing—reports, memos, briefs, etc.—if you want to keep your boss happy. If you enter a field such as education, journalism, or law, your very livelihood will depend on your ability to skillfully take pen in hand (or fingers to keyboard).

Fortunately, college is the great training ground for writing. You'll compose so many papers by the time you're done that argumentation, analysis, and the proper use of subordinate clauses will be second nature to you. Alas, the journey towards writing proficiency will be painful at times, and you'll curse the day someone invented the dreaded compare-and-contrast paper, but by the end of four years—if you put your mind to it—you'll be a pretty good writer.

You learned the basics of writing papers in high school, so I won't repeat them all here. In any case, your first college class

QUICK TIP

One of the best ways to write a better paper is to read it to yourself out loud. Hearing your words will help you catch many mistakes that your eyes have missed. It doesn't matter if people stare at you, just find a quiet spot and read through the entire paper aloud before you print out your final copy.

is likely to be composition, in which you'll go over all of it again. What I want to do instead is give you a brief professor's perspective on student papers.

ORGANIZE

Yes, it sounds boring, but a sound structure for your writing is the foundation of success. I know you received an A in Mrs. Johnson's high school creative writing class, and everyone loved your Haiku poems, but—sorry to burst your bubble—college professors don't care. Running barefoot through a meadow composing odes is all well and good, but a paper on the history of banking reform during the Roosevelt era requires a detailed plan.

The classic college paper has an introduction with your thesis statement, several supporting arguments with evidence, and a conclusion. There are lots of variations on this theme, but when in doubt, stick with it. It's simple, easy for your professor to follow, and it works.

LISTENING AND GETTING HELP

Pay particular attention to the exact assignment instructors give you. If they ask you to present three arguments for or against nuclear power, don't give them two or even four.

If they want you to single-space quotations and use footnotes instead of endnotes, do it. You'd be amazed at how many students blow their grade over technicalities like this.

Every professor you'll have in college will also have an individual style, so what worked so well with Madame Belot's French literature paper will die in Herr Schmitt's Kierkegaard seminar report. If you have any doubt whatsoever concerning the style or content of a paper, ask the professor before you begin.

Professors will often invite you to talk with them if you need any help with a paper. This is one of the surest ways to improve your paper and your grade. But, don't just go in once. Plan at least three trips to your teacher's office for any major paper—the preliminary meeting to clarify questions and plan a strategy, a second conference once you've gotten a detailed outline and a few sample paragraphs written, then a final meeting to go over your rough draft. If you give them enough time, professors are usually glad to read an entire paper informally before you turn it in officially for a grade and will often give you lots of helpful comments you can incorporate into the final product. Most students don't take advantage of this golden opportunity, but those who do are almost guaranteed a higher grade on their papers.

BE STINGY WITH WORDS

One key to writing well is eliminating unnecessary words. A clutter of superfluous adjectives, nouns, and verbs only slows down the pace of your writing and bores the reader (in this case, your professor). Here's a useful exercise—pull out the last paper you wrote and go through it with a red pen, crossing out words you don't really need. You may be surprised how much you can get rid of without harming the paper a bit. A small example:

> *The response of the candidate running for election was empty and pointless.*

A candidate by definition is someone running for office, so you don't need to state the obvious, while using both *empty* and *pointless* is an unnecessary repetition of near synonyms. Notice too that the revised sentence sounds much stronger and firmer (wait—make that just *stronger*).

This doesn't mean all your sentences should read like a newspaper headline: *Odysseus blinds Cyclops. Sails to Hades and back.* It's just that you want all your words to mean something. You may raise the objection that professors assign a set length for papers and that eliminating words only makes it harder for you to reach the required number of pages. You'd be right. Pruning words means more work for you, but nothing stands out in your writing (and hurts your grade) like weak sentences and extra paragraphs that were obviously added just to make the paper longer. I'd much rather get a slightly shorter paper full of substance than a longer one that says little. But, I've never met a paper yet which couldn't be profitably lengthened with a little extra thought and work.

SPELLING COUNTS

When I was in college, we had to write our papers by flickering candlelight on clunky manual typewriters. Well, not really, but word processors, when available, were not the magic machines they are today. But, that was an advantage in many ways, for we had to do something almost unheard of in the early twenty-first century—*we looked up words in a dictionary.* Before you start rolling your eyes like I'm your father giving you yet another speech about the good old days, consider that the spell-check function on word processing programs can give you a false sense of security. I don't know how many times I've graded papers with sentences like:

> *Their were many religious sex during Queen Victoria's rain.*

A computer only can tell if a word is listed in its dictionary file, not if it's used properly, so always proofread your work carefully with dictionary in hand. Better yet, let your roommate read it—a friend will often see mistakes that you missed.

GRAMMAR, PLEASE!

Every professor has a few sensitive spots when it comes to misusing the English language. I can, however, share a few common gripes I've heard from many different colleagues:

- Run-on sentences: Allow only one or maybe two conjunctions (*and, but, or,* etc.) per sentence. Do not string together clause after clause in an endless chain.

- Short Sentences: The opposite is also true. Repeated short sentences are jarring. They make the reader stop too often. They don't flow. Avoid them.

- Commas: These punctuation marks indicate a pause in the sentence. There are lots of complicated rules for using them, but basically insert one whenever you would need a short break while reading the sentence out loud.

- Similar Forms: Know the difference between *its* (possessive) and *it's* (contraction of *it is*). This is one of the most common errors on college papers, along with confusing *there, their,* and *they're.*

- Unclear References: Make sure your reader knows who your pronoun refers to—*If Carmen and Erin go to the cafeteria this evening, they will meet them there.* Who is *they*? Is it Carmen and Erin? What about *them*?
- Avoid Informality: A college paper is serious business, so unless you're writing dialogue for your drama class, stick with formal language. This doesn't mean you should be stuffy (*One must ponder the vicissitudes of whomsoever one addresses . . .*), but don't write as if you're simply chatting with your friends.

BE DIFFERENT (BUT ONLY IF YOU DO IT RIGHT)

Variety is the spice of life. If I assign fifty students a five-page essay on the subject of why the Roman Empire fell, most of them are likely to say it was a combination of economic and social causes ultimately leading to a weakening of the frontiers. This would be a fine answer, but after reading forty-five papers all saying the same thing, I'm ready for a change. If you can take a different angle from the rest of the class in a paper, you're more likely to impress your professors. But here's the tricky part—being different is risky, and it only works if you back up your argument very well. If you choose to argue that Rome fell solely because Christianity weakened the fighting spirit of the Romans, you will need persuasive reasoning and arguments against any potential objections. But if you can do that, I just might give you an A.

GET THEE TO THE WRITING CENTER

Almost every campus has some kind of student center dedicated to writing improvement. Here you will find professional staff, graduate students, and advanced undergraduates who can help you with everything from one-page essays to lengthy research papers. Students sometimes assume these centers are for poor writers, but this is a big mistake. Even the best writers can profit from frequent trips to these tutors. If you're having trouble with a paper on South American fruit bats or just want someone to look over your brilliant analysis of Walt Whitman's poetry, take a trip to your local writing center. After all, you're already paying for it with your tuition dollars, so why wouldn't you take advantage of the help they have to offer?

TRICKS TO FOOL YOUR PROFESSORS (THEY DON'T WORK)

Professors gathering at the faculty dining room love to regale each other with stories of students who tried to make their papers longer with no extra effort. This sort of behavior rarely works and just makes teachers use up more red ink.

A favorite trick is using large fonts (like 18 point) and extremely generous margins. The result looks something like this:

Christopher Columbus sailed from Spain and discovered the New World in 1492.

Do students really think professors won't notice how odd this looks? I've also had students manually change the pagination on lengthy research papers to skip page numbers—so that page 14, for example, is followed by page 16—hoping that a busy professor won't notice. I have to admit that this is really quite clever, and students always blame it on a software glitch, but I nail them anyway.

RESEARCH PAPERS

The *pièce de résistance* of college writing is the research paper. The very mention of this form of composition is often enough to reduce an otherwise normal student to tears. However, you really shouldn't be afraid of research papers. Yes, they're long and yes, they take a lot of work, but learning to write a great research paper is almost worth the price of tuition all by itself. It's a skill that will make or break you in any profession that requires you to thoughtfully present your work in written form.

College teachers all have different ideas about what kind of research paper they want for their particular courses, so the best rule of thumb is to pay careful attention to their instructions. But the following are some guidelines from a professor's point-of-view that are guaranteed to help you write a better paper with as little pain as possible.

CHOOSING A TOPIC

In some classes, choosing a research paper topic is easy because the professors do it for you. Even if they don't assign the whole class the same subject to write on, they'll often give you a short list of topics to choose from. With limited choices or no choice at all, you can skip this step and start your preliminary research.

Most professors, however, will allow you to pick your own topic within some broad parameters. If you are in a seminar studying the Lewis and Clark expedition, you can choose any reasonable topic dealing with that voyage of exploration—say, the representation of Native American women in the official journals or the impact of the expedition on British-American relations.

My best advice for choosing a topic is simple but crucial— *Pick a subject you care about.* I don't mean that you need a life-long passion for grizzly bears to write a paper on them, but it helps a lot if you have a genuine interest in wildlife biology. You and your research topic are going to spend a great deal of time together. As with a long road trip with a friend, it's much easier if you choose a companion you like.

One good way to start narrowing down a topic is to decide what you *don't* want to write about. If your professor tells you to write a detailed research paper on one of the levels of Hell in

Dante's *Inferno*, cross off the sins that don't really capture your imagination: blasphemy—no, forgery—nope, selling religious offices—boring, lust—well . . . maybe. You'll be surprised how fast you can pick a general topic in this way.

Don't be too specific about your topic at this point, because it may turn out that there's either not enough or too much to say about the topic—probably the latter. One of the most common mistakes students make is picking too broad a subject and being unwilling to narrow it down as the research process presses forward. A frequent experience for professors is for a student to walk into their offices and declare that they want to write a research paper on the Greek gods or the Great Depression. People have spent their lives writing multivolume works on these topics. Choosing them as a starting point is fine, but you'll want to rapidly narrow down your subject to something like *The Cult of Hermes in Archaic Athens* or *The Works Projects Administration in Northern Alabama* if you want any hope of a feasible topic.

And as always, talk with your professors. Many will require you to come in and discuss your proposed topic early in the process, but if they don't, go in anyway. A five-minute conversation with your teacher can save you days of wasted time in the library pursuing some overly ambitious or dead-end project.

PRELIMINARY RESEARCH

The next step is to look at the available sources for your topic area. Walk over to the reference section of your college library and find the general guides relating to your subject. These are books such as encyclopedias, biographical dictionaries, historical atlases, and literature handbooks that survey a topic in reasonable depth, but don't assume any specialized knowledge. The idea is to get a broad overview of your proposed topic to discover if you really want to write on it.

For example, if you are considering a paper on the historical basis for the King Arthur legend for your medieval studies class, you might begin by looking at two or three encyclopedia articles. Then go to the history reference section and see what sort of specialized guides they have on the Middle Ages. Read through any sections on King Arthur to see if historians believe there is a historical reality behind the Arthurian stories. If you find that most reputable scholars reject Arthur as pure myth, you should move on to a new topic. But if historians think there is a core of truth to the legend, then look at some of the books on King Arthur in your library. Skip the later sections discussing Arthur in troubadour romances and the Monty Python movies, and focus instead on the early sections covering late Roman Britain and Anglo-Saxon England. If you find there's enough material for a solid historical paper on King Arthur, then you're ready to frame the argument for your research paper.

THE THESIS

Professors will almost always ask you to make a strong argument in your research paper. This means that your paper cannot simply be descriptive, but must take a stand on an issue. For example:

> *Descriptive paper:* A survey of the Declaration of Independence
>
> *Thesis-driven paper:* The Declaration of Independence did not provide a society in which "all men are created equal."
>
> *Descriptive paper:* The history of genetically engineered foods
>
> *Thesis-driven paper:* Genetically engineered foods provide a safe opportunity to decrease hunger in underdeveloped countries.

It's much easier to write a descriptive paper than it is to argue a thesis, but research papers are a test of your ability to go beyond mere summary and instead argue a case. The legal analogy is actually the clearest example of what you are trying to do in a research paper—you are very much like a lawyer trying to make a credible case to a jury (in this case, your professor).

At this stage of the writing process, you don't want to produce a final thesis, but instead shape a provisional, working thesis that you can tinker with as your research progresses. Shoot for a working thesis that is narrow enough to argue within the page limits set by your professor and clearly sets forth your argument. Avoid being bland (*Air pollution is bad*), but don't be so bold that you'll have a hard time proving your case (*Wordsworth created the most moving poetry in the history of humanity*). Three examples of working theses from different disciplines could be:

> *Humanities:* Mary Wollstonecraft's "A Vindication of the Rights of Women" marked the beginning of the modern women's rights movement.
>
> *Social Sciences:* St. Patrick's Day celebrations did not begin in Ireland, but among Irish-American immigrants in Boston and New York.
>
> *Natural Sciences:* Unmanned probes provide better and cheaper scientific data than manned space flights.

You'll want to modify and expand any thesis as you conduct your research, but it's essential at this stage to have a clear idea about what your basic argument will be.

FOCUSED RESEARCH

Now that you've narrowed down the topic for your research and have formulated a working thesis, it's time to roll up your sleeves and get to work. You've already done some research in the library, but you'll need to move beyond the reference section at this point and look carefully at the books, journals, and online resources your college library has to offer.

If you haven't done so already, I recommend taking an orientation tour of your library just to find out what's available and where everything is located. Also make some time to talk with a librarian to discuss your research project. Librarians are some of the smartest and most helpful people on a college campus. They know about sources of information that most students and even professors never dreamed of. The most common question asked of any college librarian is where the bathroom is, so they'll be happy to help you with matters relating to actual books and academic resources.

Librarians can explain how to use the computer catalog, where to find scholarly journals, and how to get into the rare books room if you need to. You'll want to start by doing a computer search for all materials on your topic that could be helpful to your research. This will usually yield a stack of books and a pile of journal articles, either in print or electronic form. If your topic covers the last couple of centuries, newspaper articles can also be very helpful.

Once you've got all your sources in front of you on the table, start going though them to see if they'll be helpful or not. As you read, be sure to note down any important and useful information—*don't* assume you'll remember where it's located or you'll waste hours trying to find a crucial passage.

One of the best ways to keep track of important sources for your research is by using old-fashioned note cards. Computer files also work, but 3 x 5 cards are often easier to use when you finally sit down to write the paper. A card should contain full bibliographic information, page numbers, library call numbers, and either a direct quote or summary from the source. (If you will be making several cards from the same source, you can simplify your life by creating a single source-card with full bibliographical info, then assigning that work a number that you can use on any note cards taken from that source.) A sample card might look like the following:

> - McMaster, Carolyn. *King Arthur and the Saxon Invasions*. New York: Medieval Times Press, 2004.
> - PA 786.92
> - (page 76) Arthur may have derived from a late Roman leader named Ambrosius Aurelianus (mentioned by the sixth-century British writer Gildas).

You won't use all of your note cards when you finally write your paper, but at this stage you should treat each one as if you will.

USING ONLINE SOURCES

Ah, the wonderful Internet—all you have to do is type in a subject and you'll find dozens of websites that can help you with your research paper. And it's *so* much easier than walking all the way across campus to the library. The Internet can indeed be a great resource for your paper, but it is a realm fraught with danger. The main problem is that anyone can put anything on the web, whether they know what they're talking about or not. Any twelve-year old can create a better looking website than most Harvard professors, so the trick for you is to figure out which websites you can trust for your research.

The best place to start is with your librarian. Explain your topic and ask if the library has a list of recommended websites on that area. Academic librarians have spent a lot of hours finding reputable Internet resources on just about any subject, so why waste your time by starting from scratch?

If you move beyond Internet resources recommended by your college librarian, first find out where a website originates. A site produced by educational or government institution generally has more credibility than someone trying to sell you something or sway your opinion. Also, look for the credentials of the creators to see if they really know what they're talking about. This isn't foolproof since any wacko can claim to have a PhD (and a few do), but it's a good place to start. Also look at the tone of the website. Is it biased to some particular point of view? If so, be very careful before you take it as the truth. Corroborate any information that seems the least bit questionable. If you have any question about a site's reliability, don't use it for your research paper.

THE PERNICIOUS PROBLEM
OF PLAGIARISM

Make sure you give a citation for every quotation you use in your paper. Even if you paraphrase or just refer briefly to a source, you have to footnote it. Students will sometimes get in trouble unintentionally simply through sloppy research when they copy a passage from a book in their notes but don't record exactly where it comes from. When they put together the paper, they then include the passage without giving a reference. This makes it look as if they're trying to pass off someone else's thoughts as their own.

More deliberate forms of plagiarism are just plain foolish and will get you in serious trouble. You know those nifty Internet sites that let you download a guaranteed A paper without any work? Well, there are also sites for professors that let us quickly see if your paper is your own work. And don't even think about using an old paper from someone who took the same class last year. Professors are often absentminded, but we can usually spot a familiar paper. If we do, you will at best fail the course and at worst get kicked out of school. No matter how busy or stressed out you are, do your own work.

WRITING THE PAPER

Once you've completed your research, you're ready to put together a working draft of your paper. But don't start writing yet. Look back over your notes and consider how you want to revise your working thesis. It could be that the thesis hardly needs any changes at all, but your research may have led you to re-think your argument totally. So, sit down and construct a new thesis based on what you have learned.

You could begin writing your paper immediately, but you'll save a lot of time and trouble if you outline your arguments

QUICK TIP

Beware of using non-scholarly journals (print or on-line) in your research paper. Some professors will count off for articles from weekly news magazines and similar periodicals because they don't usually deal with a subject in sufficient depth. If you're in doubt about if a journal is scholarly or popular, ask your professor or a librarian.

and evidence first. Take your note cards, lay them all out on a table, and start to organize what you've come up with. Group together those note cards that support your thesis in different ways. For example, if you want to argue that the Trojan War really did take place, you would probably have note cards on archaeological, literary, and linguistic evidence. Look at these and see what the best way would be to organize your argument, including subgroups within each major division. Once you've done this, put everything on a page or two as a kind of map for writing your rough draft.

Now you can start to write. Apply the basic principles learned in your high school English class, but with a college research paper, make doubly sure that you organize your work in a clear manner with logical progression. Begin with your introductory paragraph containing your thesis argument, then make sure each section that follows supports that thesis:

- Introduction
- Argument One
- Argument Two
- Argument Three
- Conclusion

And, of course, include in your bibliography every work you've used in your paper. Professors will definitely mark your paper down if you cite a book in a footnote, but don't include it in your bibliography (yes, we do check).

When you've finally finished your rough draft, put it aside and go have an ice cream cone. Then come back and read through it carefully again. The key to good writing is *revision, revision, revision*. When you've done all you can, ask a friend to look at it, go over it with a peer mentor, run it by the folks at the writing center, or—best of all—ask your professor what she thinks. Consider all of this advice carefully, then write your final version.

BEFORE YOU TURN IT IN

A few final tips regarding your research paper:

- Make sure you are using your professor's preferred citation form for footnotes/endnotes and bibliography (MLA, Chicago, etc.).
- Include a cover sheet unless your professor says otherwise.
- Number your pages.
- Keep a copy of your paper.
- Print it out well before the deadline to avoid a late paper due to printer problems.

- Staple it. There's nothing more annoying than a paper with the corners folded down to hold it together.

- If at all possible, place your paper in your professor's hands rather than putting it in a mailbox or sliding it under an office door. This way you will make absolutely sure it is received.

PRESENTING YOUR RESEARCH

Once your paper is turned in, you may think your work is finally done. But many professors, especially in seminars, will ask you to give an oral presentation of your results to the class. Some students would rather walk naked across a battlefield than give a ten-minute talk to their peers, but I promise you'll be fine with a little preparation. Along with writing, public speaking is one of the most useful skills you can learn in college. There will be many times in your life when speaking to a group will be crucial, maybe even to the point of making or breaking your career. Learn to do a decent job at it and doors will open for you.

The first trick is to know your subject well. Make sure you have done a good job on your paper and reviewed it carefully several times before preparing your talk as this will give you the essential confidence to face an audience. Remember that you are going to know more about your subject than anyone in the room, with the possible exception of the professor.

You can write out your talk word-for-word, but I recommend using an outline instead. There is nothing more boring than listening to someone read a paper aloud unless they are a very polished speaker. Outlines also give you a chance to be more flexible in your presentation. But, however you proceed, be sure to practice your talk several times in front of friends before you present it to the class. Have them ask tough questions and suggest improvements, then incorporate these into your outline if you think they have merit. Feel free to use handouts or visual aids if your professor doesn't mind, but make sure these complement and illustrate your research rather than act as a distraction. And do remember that you're not in clown college. Throw in a joke if you must, but an undergraduate seminar is a professional setting, and your professor will not take kindly to humor at the expense of content.

I highly recommend taking a public speaking course while you're in college. That way you can learn an invaluable skill and get college credit for it. Whether you hope to be a doctor, lawyer, or even a college professor, the ability to present information orally to groups large and small will serve you well the rest of your life.

HOW TO STUDY
FOR A TEST

Y ou made it through high school and are going to college, so obviously you know something about how to study effectively. Those skills you learned in the past are still helpful, but college is a whole new ball game. The assignments will now come faster and contain more material than anything you've faced before. Most first-year students take at least four courses in various disciplines, but your professors are going to act as if their course is the only one you've signed up for. Your Spanish instructor is not going know that you have a history exam the same day your *Don Quixote* paper is due. Colleges are so compartmentalized that very often faculty in one department haven't the vaguest idea what's happening across campus. Even if they did, they probably wouldn't change things. This isn't because professors are cruel (in most cases), it's just that they prize their autonomy and don't like to coordinate anything with other faculty. Student rumors persist that professors secretly conspire to give all their tests on exactly the same dates. Not likely. If you could attend a typical faculty meeting, you would see that professors can rarely agree on the time of day.

So, how do you handle the heavy workloads put on you by very different professors from totally different disciplines? Try out the following techniques or adapt them to your particular style of learning—but do whatever it takes for you to master the information you need for your exams.

PAINTING A ROOM

The most successful strategy for studying that I've encountered is from students who treat studying like a home-improvement project. Have you ever painted a room red? If you try to do it in one coat, you'll have crimson globs of paint dripping everywhere, while poorly covered parts of the wall will look pink. Just as painting a wall several light coats works much better than one heavy coat, so, too, studying works much better when done in many short sessions rather than one caffeine-intensive all-nighter before the test.

PLAN AHEAD

If you're going to study for a major test several nights in a row rather than in one long session, you'll need to organize your time carefully. As mundane as it sounds, making a study chart will help you plan your available hours like nothing else. For example:

	TUESDAY	WEDNESDAY	THURSDAY	FRIDAY
6 pm	Dinner	Dinner	Dinner	*Big Spanish Exam 9 am!*
7 pm	Study Spanish Vocabulary	Study Spanish Vocabulary	Study Spanish Vocabulary	
8 pm	Study Spanish Grammar	Study Spanish Grammar	Study Spanish Grammar	
9 pm	Exercise at Gym	Exercise at Gym	Exercise at Gym	
10 pm	History Readings	Review Biology Lab	History Readings	
11 pm	Review All Spanish	Review All Spanish	Final Spanish Review	

Knowing on Tuesday afternoon that you are going to devote nine solid hours over the next few days to preparation for your Spanish exam is a powerful tool for reducing stress. Notice as well that you take a break after a couple of hours of work and that you don't neglect your other classes (a big mistake), but you've pared down studying for them to the bare minimum until the big test is over.

LAST-MINUTE REVIEWS

In the final few minutes before a test, I always see students frantically going over their notes or reviewing their Latin flash cards one last time. This is usually a mistake. If you don't know the material for a 2 P.M. test at 1:55 P.M., you're not likely to learn much in five minutes. What you'll do instead is throw yourself into a panic over all the things you suddenly realize you don't know. It's much better to take your seat, put away your books, and practice deep-breathing exercises for a few minutes before your professor hands out the exam. You'll perform much better on a test if you relax and accept that what you know is what you know—then simply do your best.

HANDWRITING

Imagine your poor professors grading twenty essay tests full of barely legible writing. Then imagine them picking up your test written in neat, easy-to-read print. Do you think you might stand a chance at a better grade than all those who are sending their teachers to the optometrist for early bifocals? If you don't know how to write quickly and neatly, practice.

TYPES OF TESTS

Professors love to give tests. It gives us a chance to see if you've actually been doing the readings and paying attention to our fascinating lectures. But the types of tests are as different as the professors who give them. Some prefer nothing but essays, while others find them a giant pain to grade. Some like to mix multiple-choice with short answer questions. If your teacher doesn't tell you what the format of an upcoming test is going to be, then ask—it's a perfectly reasonable question. How you approach a test depends largely on a professor's own style, but here are some quick tips:

- **Multiple-Choice:** If you have four choices, the standard procedure most professors follow is to make one obviously wrong and another unlikely. This leaves you two possible choices—so even if you're totally clueless, you at least have a reasonable chance of getting the answer right. Always pick an answer! You may make the wrong choice, but if you leave it blank, you'll certainly get it wrong.

- **Fill-in-the-Blank:** These are hard to fake your way through, since you either know who wrote *Moby Dick* or you don't. But, if your mind draws a complete blank, try putting down some name or term that was featured prominently in the lectures. You won't lose any points and you just might guess

correctly. If nothing else, you'll give your professor a much-needed laugh (no, it wasn't Charles
Dickens).

* **Essay:** If you've been paying attention in class, you
  can probably make a pretty good guess as to what
  the essay questions will cover. So, to prepare for
  the test, outline the answers to a few likely essay
  questions as you study. This will save you lots of
  time and anxiety.

Structure your essay answer as you would a mini-paper.
Begin with an introduction that states your thesis, then clearly
present your evidence, dividing it into short, easy-to-read paragraphs. This will make it much easier for your professor to
understand your answer. Long, rambling essays just lower your
score.

QUICK TIP

Have some fun. Those students who do best on exams
know that there's more to life than work. If you've studied hard several nights in a row for your big Shakespeare
exam and you've done everything humanly possible to
prepare yourself, then relax. Go to a movie, play football
with your friends—and finally, get a good night's sleep.

The received wisdom for essay tests among students is to write down everything possible until the professor physically pulls the test out of their hands at the end of the hour. The theory is, of course, that the more you write, the smarter you look. Unfortunately, this doesn't work. True, students who know the material well tend to write more, but adding on irrelevant facts to fill up the white space is just going to waste your professors's time and put them in a bad mood. I've read some marvelous examples of creative writing from students who obviously had no idea what the proper answer to a question was, but it never helped their grades.

MIDTERMS AND FINAL EXAMS

Few things strike fear into the heart of a college student like these exams. How can you possibly review a half or a whole semester's worth of material in a few days? You can't, of course, so concentrate on what you really need to know. Are there review sessions? Go to them. Are old exams available in the library or from a student who has taken the course? Study them carefully since professors often use the same style of questions year after year. And talk one-on-one with your professors. They will often drop hints about the kind of questions on the final, especially if you come to their office hours.

OH, WHAT A TANGLED WEB

If you would like a lecture on the moral evils of cheating, please talk to your parents. Instead, I am going to tell you why cheating in college is a horrible idea from a practical point of view:

- You may get caught. Professors see a lot more than you think, even in a large lecture hall. We know all the different techniques, from writing the answers on your shoes to texting yourself vocabulary definitions. I've also had other students in a class tell me if they saw someone cheating. And I've always taken these observations seriously.

- The risks far outweigh the benefits. In third grade, if you cheated during a social studies test and were caught, you got a scolding from the teacher and a phone call to your mom. Aside from missing your

QUICK TIP

Sometimes after performing poorly on a test, students will come to my office and ask if there is any way they can earn extra credit in the class, such as doing a book report or additional readings. A few professors out there might do this, but for most, extra credit is something you left behind in high school.

favorite TV show for a week, the consequences weren't very serious. In college, if you are caught cheating, you will fail the test at the very least and quite probably be referred to a disciplinary committee. Then, you will get to perform community service and have an ugly note posted in your records, if you're lucky. At worst, you will get kicked out of school.

♦ Even if your professors suspect you are cheating, but can't prove it, you will become the lowest of the low in their eyes. Your tests and papers will be graded with intense scrutiny and you can forget about recommendation letters. Also, we talk to other faculty members. Your reputation will precede you to your other classes.

HOW PROFESSORS GRADE

You might imagine that professors eagerly carry your tests back to their offices and begin grading right away. Unfortunately, it doesn't usually work that way. Most are teaching two or three other courses that also had tests or papers due that week, so your class exams will join the giant pile sitting on their desks. In between teaching, committee meetings, student conferences, and family responsibilities, they will try to grade all the assignments for their classes. It's not unusual to wait a week or even two before you find out your grade.

Some students will compare tests after class and complain that they unfairly received a worse grade than a friend. They will grumble that grading in the course is too subjective. While this rarely happens in fill-in-the-blank or multiple-choice tests, it's very common with longer written exams. The truth is that grading really is subjective to a certain degree—or, at least, I should say that grading is as much an art as it is a science. Of course, we look for facts and ideas gleaned from the lectures and readings, but with essay answers, especially, there is often a certain intangible quality that separates an A- from a B+. If I have fifty tests to grade that evening, I may not have sufficiently explained in my comments why your answer was a little weak, but trust me that it was.

Sometimes, students wonder if their professors are rigging the system so that only a certain number of students receive an A on a test no matter how many do well. Some professors do grade on a curve, so make sure you ask about this early in a course. On the other hand, I wouldn't know how to formulate an accurate course curve even if I wanted to. As I tell my classes on the first day, I will be thrilled to give them all A's in the course if everyone consistently earns excellent scores on tests and papers. Needless to say, this rarely happens.

HANDLING AN UNFAIR GRADE

Professors, however, are human, so occasionally we do make mistakes while grading tests. If one of your professors has goofed up, let him know—but the key is attitude. If you march into his office full of righteous anger, you'll get nowhere. Treat him with respect, and you might walk out with a higher grade.

The most frequent grading problem is simply bad math. Humanities professors are notoriously poor at addition and subtraction, so it never hurts to go back over any test to make sure we gave you the right grade. If we goofed up, just show us what we did wrong and we'll fix it. The same goes for simple mistakes. If we accidentally count you off for writing *Budapest* instead of *Bucharest*, remember that we probably were grading dozens of other tests the same day.

Differences of interpretation are more difficult to argue with your professor. If, after going carefully over your test, you honestly don't understand why your score is so low, then have a talk with your professor. She will probably explain to you why your answer was not what she was looking for, but you just might be able to convince her that your response was reasonable as well and raise your grade a few points. The more you can back up your answer with lecture notes, class readings, or outside sources, the better chance you'll have. But in the end, your professors are the final authority for their courses, so there's not going to be much you can do if they won't back down.

RECOMMENDATIONS

I n the first chapter, I mentioned one of the most important reasons for getting to know your professors is so that they can write letters of recommendation for you. But, when the time comes for you to ask a professor for a recommendation, what exactly should you do? What kind of a letter you need, who you ask, and what materials you give your professor can all make a tremendous difference in whether or not you get into the program of your dreams.

REFERENCE VERSUS RECOMMENDATION

Some application forms will not require an actual letter from a professor. They simply ask that you provide the name and contact information for several references in case they want to check up on you. These are easy, but *always ask your professors before you list them as references.* Mostly this is a matter of courtesy, but it's also essential to know we might be contacted. I've received calls from program directors asking me to comment on a student who had listed me as a reference, even though I had no idea that student was applying for anything. We can do a much better job of bragging about you if we have some warning about your application ahead of time.

TYPES OF RECOMMENDATIONS

You will need recommendation letters for just about any program you apply to during or after college. Scholarships, summer internships, and study-abroad programs are the most common type of letters you'll need in your early college years—and some of these will come up even during your first or second semester. If you want to compete for an academic scholarship for sophomore music majors or study Hindi in India next July, you will almost certainly need two or three letters from professors who are familiar with you and your work.

Later, in their senior years, many students will be applying for graduate and professional programs. You might apply for anything from business to veterinary school, but all of these will need thoughtful and supportive letters from faculty members. This is when the rule of getting to know your professors will really pay off.

WHOM TO ASK

Students are sometimes hesitant to ask a professor for a letter of recommendation, but I can assure you that it is one of the most enjoyable duties we have as college teachers. Yes, it takes a little time from our busy schedules, but it's a privilege to write a letter for a student who has done well in our courses. So don't worry that you might be bothering a favorite professor when you request a recommendation. With rare exception, we'll be glad to do it.

Whom you should ask for a letter depends on what type of recommendation you need. If you're applying for a January program to study penguins in Antarctica, you should ask a science teacher who knows you well. If you want to become a rabbi, go to a professor who can speak to your abilities as a scholar and leader. The trick is to ask whoever is most appropriate for whatever program you want to get into. In all cases, pick someone who actually knows something about you and your work. The worst thing you can do is ask for a letter from a professor who barely knows you. If you do, you're likely to get a short, uninformative recommendation that will not impress anyone.

For the really big recommendations—medical, law, and graduate school you want to be very careful whom you ask. These recommendations are going to go a long way toward making or breaking your future plans, so pick professors who know you very well and who are enthusiastic about your abilities. It will be especially impressive to committees if that professor can say she has known and worked with you for several years rather than just a semester or two.

HOW TO ASK

Most professors will be flattered to write a recommendation, so the best approach is simply to ask them upfront. If, for some reason, they are hesitant or refuse your request, then just thank them and be glad they didn't say yes. The last thing you want is some tepid or damaging recommendation letter.

But, most professors will be happy to oblige you. You should, however, give them more than just a required form. Include a description of the program you're applying for, a resume summarizing your course work, honors, and activities, and any appropriate supporting materials—especially those that directly relate to your performance in any course you've taken with that professor. You may remember well your brilliant research paper three years ago on Polynesian mythology, but your professor has graded a few thousand other papers since then and has probably forgotten yours. Just include a copy of it among the materials you give to your teacher. This will let him be much more specific about your accomplishments when he writes his letter. Don't go overboard, but including a few impressive papers or other examples of your worthiness never hurts.

You may wonder what your professors will say about you, but if you've chosen your writers well, you should trust them. There's usually a box you can check off at the top of a recommendation form in which you give up your right to ever see your professor's letter. You should agree to this. Professors will feel more confident to write even a glowing letter if they know it will remain between them and the admissions committee.

Committees do get tired of reading what seem like form letters praising a student—*John is an excellent student. He earned an A in my course.* This is why any materials you can give your professors to remind them of your achievements is important. I always try to spice up my letters a little with positive personal comments and anecdotes supporting the student's abilities. I once even wrote a letter for a student applying to a prestigious law school that began with the usual listing of good grades and stellar performance, but then ended it as follows:

> *Samuel is extremely bright, very hard working, and would be an asset to any law school program. But, he is so persistent that if we were trapped together on a desert island, I would probably strangle him. On the other hand, if I'm ever in real trouble someday, he's the one I'm calling to be my attorney.*

I'm happy to say he was admitted with a full scholarship and is now a successful lawyer.

FOLLOW UP

I'd like to say that all professors write recommendation letters in a timely manner, but it just doesn't happen. If the deadline for letters is fast approaching and your teacher still hasn't gotten one in, it is perfectly appropriate for you to gently and respectfully remind him to get busy. With your future on the line, you can't afford to be shy about nudging old Professor McDonald to get the letter in the mail. If he doesn't, you could spend a year flipping burgers while you wait to reapply.

THE TOP TEN WAYS TO ANNOY YOUR PROFESSORS

No college student sets out to deliberately offend professors—it would be crazy to spend so much money, then anger the people who hold your grades in their hands. Yet, every year countless students make very avoidable mistakes that only end up hurting their standing with their teachers. You can probably avoid most of these blunders by using common sense, but pointing them out may help you sail through your college years more smoothly.

10. SPECIAL TESTS

Accidents, sickness, and family emergencies happen to every-one, including students. At some point in college, a crisis will hit you on the same day you have a major test. Most professors are very understanding *if* you have a legitimate reason for need-ing a make-up exam. If, however, you want to schedule a spe-cial test because you slept through your alarm or will be leaving on a road trip with your friends, you will not score any points with your professor by asking for special consideration. When you request an exam separate from the rest of the class, you're really asking professors to sit down and write a completely dif-ferent test for you, then take time out of their busy schedules to administer it. If you're seriously ill or there's a major problem, of course we'll do it. But you'll need a very good reason.

9. TAP, TAP, TAP

This really falls under classroom etiquette, but you'd be sur-prised how many students unconsciously do something mad-dening in class, especially during the silence of a test. During an exam a few years ago, one student repeatedly tapped the end of his ballpoint pen against his wooden desk while he pon-dered an essay question. The noise resounded off the walls of the old lecture hall like a rifle shot. He had no idea he was doing it until he looked up at me and the entire class staring daggers at him. Bang, sniff, crunch, or wheeze, watch out for annoying behaviors that will make your professor and everyone else want to toss you out the door.

8. I'M PAYING YOUR SALARY

Students are rarely so crude that they say this to a professor, even if they are justifiably angry, but most professors have heard it at least once during their careers. The truth is that even if you are paying full tuition at a college, a large portion of the tab is still picked up by other sources, but that's really beside the point. If you're foolish enough to say this to a college teacher, she will probably sneer at you and say, "Oh, you're the one. Well then, let's talk about a raise."

7. MY OTHER CLASSES ARE MORE IMPORTANT

You'd be surprised how often professors hear this from struggling students. An art history major walks into the office of a biology professor and says, "I'm only taking your class to fill my science requirement, and I've got to focus this semester on the Michelangelo seminar required for my major. Can't you cut me some slack on the exam?" The professor's answer is always, "No, of course not." Sorry, but your motives for taking a class are irrelevant. The fact is you signed up for it, so you have to do the same work as everyone else. If you can't, then drop the course.

6. I JUST CAME DOWN WITH DIPHTHERIA

If you need extra time on a paper or miss an exam, it's always best to tell your professor the truth when requesting an extension or a make-up test. College campuses are like small towns where everybody knows everyone else's business. If you forgot about a physics exam and tell your professor you missed it because you were in the infirmary having your tonsils removed, chances are your teacher plays squash with a doctor there who will blow your cover. I've had students claim they couldn't turn in a paper because they were in bed with the flu, just to see them working out at the gym that same afternoon. Besides, most professors have developed a finely honed ability to detect dishonesty. The truth may be painful and it may earn you a scolding from your professor, but lying will get you in much worse trouble in the end.

5. I NEED MORE TIME

Regarding extensions for papers, don't ask for one unless you really, truly need it. At the end of every semester when final papers are due, I brace myself for the flood of requests for more time. Even though I assigned the paper three months ago, there's always a substantial group of students who don't start until the last minute. Of those, at least half will not finish on time and will plead for an extension. I even created an official-looking form once with boxes to check for the most common excuses (my computer is down, I'm having a personal crisis with my girlfriend/boyfriend, etc.). Grading late papers is a royal pain for professors, so try very hard to make their deadlines.

4. MY GRADE DOESN'T REFLECT MY EFFORT

Professors frequently hear this lament. Tearful students come to our offices after a midterm and explain that they studied the material faithfully and carefully, but still did poorly on the test. Often they didn't really study as hard as they imagine, but sometimes they genuinely tried their very best and still did poorly. My heart always goes out to these students, because I had similar experiences in college. Most of the time they just need to work on their study skills, so I always do my best to suggest techniques appropriate to the course. But in the end, there's a painful truth everyone needs to realize about professors and grades: *We don't judge your efforts, just your results.* There is no way we can know how many hours you spent in the library preparing for a test. We can't get inside your head to see how much you could have included in your term paper, but didn't. All we can evaluate you on is the written evidence you give us.

3. DID I MISS ANYTHING IMPORTANT?

Here's a scenario that has happened to me and every other college teacher more times than I can count. At the end of a lecture, a student will approach me and say, "Hey professor, I was absent all last week because my cousin back in New Jersey was in the county Little League championship" or something similar. Then they ask the one question you should never ask a professor: *Did I miss anything important?* I'm always tempted to say, "Important? Not really, I was just up here talking carefully prepared nonsense to myself." Instead I bite my tongue and suggest they get the class notes from a fellow student and see me if they have any further questions. But, that student has earned a mental black mark that may well come back to haunt him when I'm calculating borderline grades at the end of the course.

2. I FORGOT WE HAD AN APPOINTMENT

Some students are particularly bad about making appointments with professors then not showing up. They forget to mark it in their calendars, something else comes up, or they just blow it off. I suppose they think professors are always in their offices anyway and don't really care if they skip an arranged meeting. Wrong. We're glad to meet with you, but it often means rearranging another appointment, rushing back from lunch, or staying late at work. I've postponed auto repairs and missed my son's kindergarten choir recital to meet with students who never showed up.

If you make an appointment, write it down. If you can't make a meeting, call the professor as quickly as possible. Common courtesy goes a long way to getting—and staying—in the good graces of your teachers.

1. WILL THAT BE ON THE TEST?

This number-one faux pas can be a reasonable question *if you ask it the right way.* Professors get do get tired of being asked again and again during class if something will be on the exam, as if they were teaching a drivers license prep course. We like to think that students are interested in the subject first and their grades second. This is idealistic, but play along and you'll keep us happy.

Though it's perfectly logical to inquire what a professor expects you to know for an exam, *never ask the question directly in front of the whole class.* It makes you look like a shallow grade-monger to everyone, especially your teacher. Instead, ask about testable material after class or during office hours. Even then be a little discrete. Don't blurt out, "Will this be on the test?" Ease into the question with something like, "Professor Smith, I really enjoyed your lecture on seismology today, but I was wondering if we'll need to trace the San Andreas fault on a map for the exam?" Professors will usually appreciate the practical nature of the question and be as helpful as they can if you ask tactfully. After all, we used to be students too.

HANDLING
PROBLEMS

No matter how hard you work in college, no matter how faithfully you follow the advice in this handbook, there are going to be times in your life when everything falls apart. Sometime you will be overwhelmed by four research papers all due on the same day. Sometime you or someone you love will experience a serious personal crisis that requires immediate attention, no matter how many exams you have that week. When this happens, remember the third rule: *Talk to your professors.* Many students in difficult situations simply disappear without a word during a crisis, only to re-emerge days or weeks later when it's too late to work through the problem. Not every problem can be easily fixed, but I guarantee it won't get fixed at all unless you sit down and work it out with your professors.

YOUR CREDIBILITY ACCOUNT

When you sign up for a class with a new professor, it's like beginning a baseball game—you step up to the plate with no hits and no strikes against you. Your professors don't know that you're a wonderful, trustworthy person who loves small animals and would gladly return a lost wallet full of money to its owner—so it's going to be your job to prove it to them. Every time you show up for class well-prepared and eager to answer questions you will earn a little gold star in that professor's mental grade-book. Every time you skip class or do poorly on an exam you will earn just the opposite. When crisis time does hit you—as it will everyone at some time in college—you are going to wish mightily you had nothing but gold stars by your name.

It's simple human nature. If you go to your professor with a serious difficulty—let's say you were just diagnosed with mono and need extra time on a paper—that teacher is much more likely to be helpful to someone who has earned a high degree of credibility in his eyes than someone who has shown little interest in the course. If you're a good student who has obviously tried hard in a class, it's likely your professor will believe you and reach out to help when you claim your car suddenly died on the freeway while you were taking your sick cat to the vet. Keep your credibility account high, and it will smooth over many potential problems with your professors.

FALLING BEHIND

This is the most common crisis faced by college students. You started out the semester just fine. You kept up with all the readings, did well on the first few quizzes, and earned high marks on your papers. But, then the assignments started to come faster and faster. Physics labs piled on top of Russian verb lists and choir practice, until you just couldn't keep up any more. By midterm exams, your grades crashed and what had promised to be a great semester has turned into a nightmare.

The first thing you should do when this happens is shift into emergency mode and make an appointment right away with any professor whose class you're having difficulty with. Don't beg and plead, but calmly explain that you're overwhelmed and would appreciate any advice on how to improve your performance in their classes. After—or preferably during—this process, take a hard, cold look at what you can cut out of your schedule to make extra study time. Do you really need to work with five service organizations off campus every weekend? Can you afford to cut back some hours from your job in the library? Do you really need to sleep? Just kidding, though I'll bet you can find at least an hour or two a day that you can devote to playing serious catch-up in your courses. It won't be fun for a month or two, but in the end it will pay off.

ILLNESS

College dormitories are a wonderful breeding ground for disease. Take hundreds of stressed-out students surviving on nothing but pizza and make them share a tiny space with communal bathrooms and poor ventilation—voila, you've got a human petri dish for every kind of respiratory and digestive disorder you can imagine. Of course, you should do everything you can to avoid such troubles—get plenty of rest, eat right, wash your hands frequently—but try as you might, you'll probably catch whatever illness is going around.

The most important thing when sickness strikes in college is to take care of your health. You're not doing your professors or fellow students any favor by dragging yourself to class and spreading germs around. Instead, immediately go to the campus health center. When you get back to your room, email or call your professors, and let them know what's going on. Emphasize that you will be in to see them about any missed work as soon as you can walk again without fainting. When that's done, kick out your noisy roommate, have a bowl of chicken soup, and go to bed.

DEATH IN THE FAMILY

The hardest college crisis of all is when someone close to you is terminally ill or dies. The last thing you want to think about at such a time is schoolwork, but the unfortunate truth is that college goes on even in the middle of your grief. Almost all professors will go out of their way to work with you and grant you extensions for your work, but you need to contact them as soon as possible. As difficult as it is, call them immediately and explain your situation. If you need extra time to finish a project or paper, just tell them. If you are in a situation where you need to go home for an indefinite period to be with your family, talk with your professors, and also meet with someone in the dean's office or counseling center to find out what the school's policy is on extended absences.

My father became seriously ill and passed away when I was an undergraduate. Years later, I am still grateful to my professors who worked with me to make up a whole month of missed classes that semester. I would be very surprised if yours would not do the same for you.

INTERNATIONAL
AND
NONTRADITIONAL
STUDENTS

T he advice in this book is meant to be useful to anyone entering college, but there are plenty of students on the first day of class who don't fit the mold of a typical freshman whose parents just dropped them off in the family minivan. These students come from outside the country or perhaps they are older than average, maybe much older. International students and older adults can succeed wonderfully in college, but they can face special challenges in the classroom. It has been my privilege to teach many students in both categories over the years, so I would like to offer a few pointers to the particular circumstances they face in academic life.

INTERNATIONAL STUDENTS

As if beginning college weren't stressful enough, try doing it in a foreign country in a culture that may be vastly different from your own. Throw in a different language and a thousand unwritten rules of behavior you're expected to follow and it's no wonder international students can find the transition difficult. But, some of the best, brightest, and most successful students I've ever taught come from beyond our borders.

Classroom dynamics vary in different countries. In some cultures, students are expected to keep quiet and carefully write down everything their teachers say. Most American colleges encourage a more interactive experience between students and professors. This can take some getting used to, but don't be afraid to jump in and participate. Of course, you should be respectful of your professors, but don't be afraid to ask questions and offer your reasoned opinion on the topic of the day.

On the other hand, you may sometimes need to remind other students (or even professors) that you cannot speak for the whole world. If you are in political science class and someone asks you how people abroad view something, please do tell them what you think, but point out that the world is a big place. I would imagine even within your own family back home there are differences of opinion on many issues.

And at the risk of repeating myself, please talk to your professors if you have any questions about papers, tests, or anything else concerning their courses. We know it can be difficult adjusting to college in a foreign country, and we do want to help you in any way we can.

OLDER STUDENTS

If you remember disco lights and leisure suits, you probably have a few more years behind you than most new college students. Life in the classroom over the age of twenty-five (or forty or seventy) has its own challenges, but rest assured that it can be a wonderful experience for you.

I have enjoyed teaching many older adult students, from returning veterans and young parents retooling for a new career to eighty-year-old grandmothers earning the degree they

> **QUICK TIP**
> If you are from overseas, make sure you become familiar with your school's international student office. They can be of immense help in practical matters such as visas and work regulations, and they can also be a great source of emotional and social support. Also, consider hooking up with a host family. It can be a great way to learn about local culture and find a home away from home.

always dreamed of. Such nontraditional students are invariably hard-working and conscientious, a real joy to have in class. They carefully prepare the assignments, participate energetically in discussions, and rarely miss class because they were out late partying. But, there are challenges unique to older students.

If you are sitting in a class surrounded by eighteen-year-olds, you are probably a little worried. What will the others in the class think of you? Will the professor expect you to know all the answers? Are you wearing shoes that went out of style before the Berlin Wall fell?

So let's be honest—you're not a kid anymore, nor should you try to act like one. The students in your class obviously can see that you're older than they are, but most of them couldn't care less. They are focused on organic chemistry or metaphors in Milton's poetry, not on you. They will quickly accept you as one of the gang if you just be yourself.

But, do be careful not to dominate the classroom conversation. Your years have given you an important perspective that can be valuable to the course, but students will not appreciate it if you begin every comment with "I remember when." Share your insights, by all means, but respect the fact that the younger crowd has much to contribute as well. You can learn a great deal from people half your age if you give them a chance.

And as always, if you have special concerns or circumstances, speak to the professor. If you have to miss class because of a sick child or prostate exam, just let them know. By the way, if your childcare falls through at the last minute, the professor might not mind if you bring a well-behaved child to school. If they can draw quietly with crayons and not bother anyone, I would have no objections. I once brought my infant daughter to my Roman history class when the babysitter cancelled. She slept like an angel most of the time. When she finally got fussy, I simply picked her up and continued my lecture on military policy under Caesar Augustus, while holding her in my arms.

No matter what your age, the life of a college student is always challenging. Everyone feels out of place sometimes, but with a little perseverance and a lot of hard work, you'll be just fine.

conclusion

Success in college is not about beating the system—it's about learning skills that will help you thrive in a very difficult environment. College is intense and demanding. It is also one of the greatest opportunities you'll ever have to discover new worlds and new ideas. Always keep these ideals in mind when you're trying to master the skills of writing, test-taking, and working with your professors. What a waste it would be to learn how to ace an astronomy course without appreciating the wonders of the universe.

That being said, I've tried, in this brief book, to give you a very practical guide to dealing with college professors and their demands on you. But, there are many other excellent works which can help you succeed during your college career. A few of my favorites are below.

COPING WITH COLLEGE

Still stressed out about college? I recommend *Getting the Best Out of College* by Peter Feaver, Sue Wasiolek, and Anne Crossman with plenty of good advice from a professor, dean, and student. Also, look at *College Rules!* by Sherrie Nist-Olejnik and Jodi Patrick Holschuh. Finally, Harlan Cohen's *The Naked Roommate* has great advice on residence halls, relationships, and the weird side of college life.

WRITING

Every college student should own and treasure a copy of William Strunk and E.B. White's short *The Elements of Style*, full of pithy advice for all writers such as "Prefer the standard to the offbeat" and "Make every word tell." White wrote *Charlotte's Web*, for goodness sake, and you never see Wilbur the pig wasting any words. Also a gem, is the veteran journalist William Zinserr's *On Writing Well*, a guide to all varieties of engaging prose from travel memoirs to science and technology. If you don't know the difference between *its* and *it's*, rush out immediately to buy a copy of Lynne Truss' (or is it Truss's?) hilarious and informative guide to punctuation, *Eats, Shoots, and Leaves*.

PARENTS

College is hard for you, but it's no picnic for your family either. Endless bills, separation anxiety, and guilt over converting your old bedroom to a sewing room—parents have a lot to deal with. A great book for you to buy your folks before you leave is *Letting Go: A Parents' Guide to Understanding the College Years* by Karen Levin Coburn and Madge Lawrence Treeger. It will make your life easier, too.

index